"Honey, Hang in There!"

Other books by Sandra Picklesimer Aldrich

Bless Your Socks Off
From One Single Mother to Another
HeartPrints (with Bobbie Valentine)
Men Read Newspapers, Not Minds
Will I Ever Be Whole Again?
101 Upward Glances
Bible Encounters: 21 Stories of Changed Lives (with
    Thomas Youngblood)

"Honey, Hang in There!"

Encouragement for Busy Moms

Sandra Picklesimer Aldrich

Fleming H. Revell
A Division of Baker Book House Co
Grand Rapids, Michigan 49516

© 2003 by Sandra Picklesimer Aldrich

Published by Fleming H. Revell
a division of Baker Book House Company
P.O. Box 6287, Grand Rapids, MI 49516-6287
www.bakerbooks.com

Printed in the United States of America

Published in association with the literary agency of Alive Communications, Inc., 7680 Goddard Street, Suite 200, Colorado Springs, Co., 80920.

Library of Congress Cataloging-in-Publication Data is on file at the Library of Congress, Washington, D.C.

ISBN 0-8007-5833-1

Most of the names have been changed to respect the privacy of the individuals.

Published in association with the literary agency of Alive Communications, Inc., 7680 Goddard Street, Suite 200, Colorado Springs, Colorado 80920.

To Holly and Eric Hulen and their son,
Luke Anthony—

who would still be the world's most precious,
clever, and all-around delightful little boy
even if he weren't my grandson

Contents

Acknowledgments

Special thanks to the Revell/Baker editorial team, especially Vicki Crumpton, whose flexibility was helpful as I pulled together this book during yet another family crisis. I wish Vicki lived closer to Colorado Springs; she'd be a great buddy with whom to explore everything from antique shops to western canyons. I am also grateful to Mary Suggs, editor, and Wendy Wetzel, assistant editor, for their attention to manuscript details. And to Mim Pain, president of WorkPlace Influence, whose constant encouragement includes letting me whine about deadlines, travel schedules, and goofy relatives during evening walks. Thanks too for Bonnie McGowan's patience as she decoded my scribbles to input endless changes in the text. And, as always, I have great appreciation for Greg Johnson of Alive Communications, Inc., in Colorado Springs, who was a friend long before he became my agent.

Thanks to all of you who have been my ongoing cheerleaders.

Dear Busy Mom

I'm typing this letter to you on a beautiful Colorado morning. I'm sitting in my organized home office. Through the open window, I can hear the birds greeting the dawn. My house is clean. My house is quiet. My house is empty.

My children, Jay and Holly, are married. And I'm wondering how we arrived at this stage so soon. Wasn't it just yesterday I was in the thick of an endless round of zipping snowsuits, buckling car seats, wiping noses, and bandaging knees? And then the next week, it seemed, I was helping collect bugs for school projects. But just as I found the calligraphy pen so they could print the identification labels, both children had turned into teenagers asking to borrow the car and talking about college. One stage swirled into the next, and suddenly I was an empty nester. Oh, sure, during those busy days of caring for children, I couldn't comprehend that the chaos would actually come to an end.

But here I am, just as—believe it or not—you will be too. So come along while I share some of the experiences that brought me to this point. I'm no child-rearing expert, so please don't expect me to offer "Ten Ways to

Produce Perfect Children." Just let me encourage you with my zany experiences, honest confessions, and practical hints. And as you read, remember, I'm a veteran mother who remembers and understands—and who would gladly do it again if given the choice.

Sandra Picklesimer Aldrich

1

As Different as Night and Day

*For you created my inmost being; you knit me together in
my mother's womb.*

Psalm 139:13

My two children, Jay and Holly, are sixteen and a half
months apart. (I add the "half" because I desperately
needed those last two weeks of sleep before Holly arrived!)
Their closeness in age shows God's sense of humor.
You see, two of my siblings were born within eighteen months of each other, and I once self-righteously
declared, "*My* children will never be eighteen months
apart!"

Well, they're *not.*

What I remember most about those early years of
mothering can be summarized in one word: exhaustion.
Adding to the weary excitement was the fact that Jay and
Holly were (and are!) as different as night and day. Before
they were born, their unique personalities were already
evident. Jay started running in the womb. He kicked my

ribs, poked my bladder, and, it seemed, braced his feet against my hip bones as he stretched against my lungs until I thought I'd never get a full breath again. Whenever we attended noisy family gatherings, he'd become even more active, as though he were yelling through my navel, "Let me out! I have an opinion on that too!"

Holly, on the other hand, liked finding a comfortable spot under my heart and settling in for hours—even days. After Jay's prenatal running, I'd start to worry about this new baby and think maybe something was wrong. I'd try pushing against my side. Nothing. Then in a panic, I'd thump my side to make her move so I could assure myself she was all right. She'd jump, just as though she were yelling, "What?!"

Whew. The baby's all right, I'd think, my worry lessened for a few more days.

Uh, Holly's now a little nervous in life. Once, I told her she had to stop worrying so much. Then, trying to spiritualize the situation, I counseled: "You've got to give this to God."

She nodded, then said, "I know that, Mom. But I'll be going along just fine, and suddenly it's as though somebody hits me alongside the head!"

Oh, dear. They *do* remember.

An Encouraging Hug

Honey, even children born into the same family will be as different as night and day.

2

Just Who Was Lost Again?

The LORD will keep you from all harm—he will watch over your life; the LORD will watch over your coming and going both now and forevermore.

Psalm 121:7–8

My children brought their prebirth personalities into the world, and I soon had one child whom I couldn't find and another whom I couldn't lose (not that I tried). Holly would walk so close to me I'd almost trip, but I lost Jay so many times I was on a first-name basis with the security guard at the local shopping mall. The first announcement over the public address system was, "Will the parents of a little boy with blond hair, a yellow sweatshirt, and blue jeans please come to security to claim him?" Over the following weeks, those pleas escalated into, "Will *Jay's* mother please come to security?"

And, of course, when I showed up—frantic and apologetic—Jay would shake his head at me and say, "Where *were* you?" As though *I* were the one who had been lost!

I wish I'd been confident enough to buy one of those splendid safety halters parents attach to their children, but my mother-in-law disparagingly called them "leashes."

At least those parents don't lose their kids, I'd think.

If I had to do it over again, though, you'd better believe I'd have a safety harness on Jay. Pride—and worrying about what others think—has no place in our thoughts when it comes to keeping our children safe.

An Encouraging Hug

Honey, don't worry about what others think or say.
Keep your children safe.

3

Shopping Cart Adventures

If any of you lacks wisdom, he should ask God, who gives generously to all without finding fault, and it will be given to him.

James 1:5

Grocery shopping with two little people was an adventure. To keep from losing toddler Jay, I'd plop him down into the cart, where he'd take a commandeering stance and wave his arms toward the cookies. Then I'd position Holly in the cart seat—supported by a small pillow—and, to keep her from crying, lean toward her to assure her I hadn't abandoned her. So there we were: the two-and-a-half-year-old trying to reach everything on the shelves, his baby sister hanging on to a lock of my hair, and me—the tired mother—walking lopsided, trying to keep the cart in the middle of the aisle.

Occasionally other shoppers would glance at me as though wondering, *Why doesn't she control those kids?*

And I'd think, *They* are *controlled. You ought to see them when they're not!*

Invariably, our little trio would be spotted by a grandmother-type who would smile, pat me on the arm, and say, "Oh, honey, these are the best days of your life!"

If I heard that two or three times before rolling up to the dairy section, I'd be frantic and think, *If these are the best years, what are the rest like?*

Somehow we all survived those adventures, and today Jay and Holly are grown. Now when I go to the grocery store, I can steer as closely as I want to the cookies and sugar cereals, knowing that only those items I choose will land in the cart. And occasionally I see tired young mothers walking lopsided and steering a cart containing a commandeering toddler and a whimpering little one.

Now it's *my* turn to smile and pat them on the arm! And I say, "Hang in there, honey! It does get better!"

Never have I been told to mind my own business. The response is always, "Oh, thank you! Thank you!"

And, truly, less exhausting days do come.

An Encouraging Hug

Honey, these exhausting days will pass.

4

Cleaning Ladies Are Biblical

She gets up while it is still dark; she provides food for her family and portions for her servant girls.

Proverbs 31:15

If I could choose to do anything over, it would be to enjoy my children moment by moment. But there was so much work to do that I wondered if something was wrong with me because I found many aspects of mothering *exhausting*. The relatives, my church, and even the TV ads emphasized only the soft, cuddly aspects. And those, indeed, are wonderful. But I was too sensitive to the expectations of others and too uptight to laugh at the ridiculousness of trying to raise two "perfect" children. I wish I had given myself permission to relax and have fun. But I had relatives who always commented on how nice my house looked and friends who looked forward to our hosting the Bible study.

I wish I had known it was okay to be tired—and that having a cleaning lady in every two weeks was not only common sense but actually *biblical.* Look at Proverbs 31:15 again: "She gets up while it is still dark; she provides food for her family and portions for her servant girls." *Portions for her servant girls?* The Perfect Proverbs Woman had servants! So get a cleaning lady! (And if *you* are a cleaning lady, may God especially bless you!)

Let me say it again: Get help. Don't allow exhaustion to cause you to miss the joy of these moments. A loving environment is more important to your child than how spotless the house is. But if you're like me and can't relax when things are in chaos, allow me to nudge you to rethink your "gotta do everything myself" mind-set.

If it isn't feasible for you to get a cleaning lady, what about hiring a high school student to help you for a couple of hours each week? Or pairing up with a friend to help clean each other's home? Work, including housecleaning, goes much faster when folks share the load. In the Kentucky farming community of my youth, neighbors helped each other harvest a crop or paint a barn or put up the produce. The old adage "Many hands make light work" is true. We've heard it countless times before, but it's a good reminder of what is truly important: Children spell *love* T-I-M-E.

An Encouraging Hug

Honey, find ways to enjoy your children more—even if it means hiring a cleaning lady.

5

Wishing Away Today

Therefore do not worry about tomorrow, for tomorrow will worry about itself. Each day has enough trouble of its own.

Matthew 6:34

I once saw a wall hanging I should have purchased: *Normal day, let me be aware of the treasure you are.* This truth is too often forgotten in our daily schedules.

I remember the story of one mother who was at the airport with her fresh-out-of-high-school son. He was on his way to six weeks of boot camp. As he reminded her, "I won't be able to write much, but don't worry," she kept wondering what had happened to the years; her little boy was now a man. It seemed as though just last week she had brought him home from the hospital—covered with newborn wrinkles and that mop of black hair. During those early weeks, he had been a poor sleeper. Her one thought was *I can't wait until he's sleeping through the night.*

Finally, that milestone arrived. But he was a high-energy toddler who was always into things. Her goal changed to *I can't wait until he's in school.* When school came, her kitchen windowsill was covered with plastic cups sprouting beans and carrot tops. *I can't wait until he's in middle school,* she thought. Well, when middle school came, she couldn't wait until he was a mature high schooler. And suddenly he had graduated and was leaving for the military.

Now, there she was, sitting in an airport with him, crying because she had wished so intently for the next stage that she had lost any joy in the present one.

An Encouraging Hug

Honey, today is a treasure, and so are you.

6

Cooling Off

*Therefore, as God's chosen people, holy and dearly loved,
clothe yourselves with compassion, kindness, humility,
gentleness and patience.*

Colossians 3:12

I remember one hot, sticky morning in Michigan. My husband, Don, was chairman of the church deacon board and had invited the men to our home for that evening's meeting. But he forgot to tell me until that morning. In typical style, though, he said before going out the door, "But don't go to a lot of trouble. Just put out chips and dip."

I'm from Kentucky; I don't do just chips and dip. So I became a woman on a mission. I made—from scratch—oversized pastry puffs and stuffed them with spicy meat I thought the men would like. (Young mothers, hear me: Nobody with young children—and in her right mind—makes her own pastry puffs!)

I also cleaned the entire house, even though the men would be only in the dining room. After all, one of the men might get lost and wander upstairs and, looking for the meeting, open the linen closet and discover that my towels were not stacked by color. One of them might open the oven door and see the boiled-over remains of last night's dinner. Worse yet, one might open the silverware drawer and discover I had crumbs in with the forks!

So with an intense day ahead, I put my two toddlers into the fenced-in backyard with this command: "Mama's really busy today, so don't get your clothes wet!"

The day before, they had discovered the outside faucet and joyfully dumped water into their sandbox, concocting sand "towns" surrounded by lakes in which floated twig inhabitants. That was a wonderfully creative activity for toddlers—but did I appreciate it? Oh, no! Because whenever Holly got even a spot of water on her little shirt, she'd trudge into the house, whimpering about being wet. I'd have to change her entire outfit before she'd go outside again. (Even at two, she had to "match"—not because I said so but because *she* said so!) Jay, on the other hand, thrived on being covered with wet sand and would complain if I wrestled him out of his clothes.

The day before, the activity had kept them busy for an entire afternoon, so I'd put up with it. But on this particular morning, I didn't have time to worry about changing toddlers' clothes.

About twenty minutes into my best-laid plans, I was right in the middle of polishing something (probably the *back* of the TV) when I heard water running. I muttered something about "those kids" disobeying my orders and then looked out the open window, ready to yell. To my amazement, two *stark naked* toddlers were standing next to their sandbox hosing each other down! Holly's clothes were folded neatly by the fence (yes, even at two) while Jay's were scattered all over the yard.

Within seconds I was charging out the door. Did I say, "Oh, you clever children! Mama told you not to get your clothes wet, so you took them off"?

No? You got that right! I raced toward them, screaming the ridiculous question, "What are you doing?" (Why do we ask dumb questions? The only one that tops that is "Do you want a spanking?!")

Jay had been hosing down his little sister, but at the sound of my voice, he turned and saw a crazy woman coming toward him. There was nothing to do but hose her down!

Then that boy had the good sense to drop the hose and run. There I was, soaking wet and chasing a naked toddler around our backyard—in full view of the neighbors, who had been enjoying a quiet bit of gardening until that moment.

Jay still remembers that morning. In fact he says it's a good thing I didn't catch him until I was too tired to do anything!

An Encouraging Hug

Honey, some of your most frustrating parenting moments now are going to make great stories later on.

7

The Pretty Jungle

You are worried and upset about many things, but only one thing is needed.

Luke 10:41–42

Even with the lesson learned from that day of being hosed down, I still was a slow learner. Just a few mornings later, I was rushing—again—to cross things off my eternal "to do" list. The first item was to get the letters to the corner mailbox before the early pickup. But hurrying two toddlers along a sidewalk teeming with wondrous things to look at was impossible. Jay was fascinated by the ants scurrying across the concrete, so he'd get on his hands and knees to watch them. As his little sister joined him, Jay would exclaim in his three-and-a-half-year-old voice, "Holly, look at that ant carrying the big crumb! That's like you or me picking up a car with our teeth."

Holly, ignoring such scientific wonders, would coo, "Oh, is that a daddy ant or a mommy ant?"

Where was I? About ten feet ahead, saying, "Come on. Hurry up."

Eventually we made it to the mailbox and then started back. Since I had a long list of things to do, I wanted to hurry home, so we walked through the vacant lot. The neighborhood children rode their bikes through this shortcut on their way to school. The wheels had worn a wide path through the waist-high weeds, and this route would get us home sooner.

Calling, "Hurry up, you two," I rushed across the lot, ignoring the Queen Anne's lace, black-eyed Susans, and blue cornflowers on either side of me. When I reached the sidewalk, I turned back to call another command, but the scene before me stifled the words. Toddler Jay was holding his little sister's hand as they gazed upward at the flowering weeds over their heads. Then, his voice filled with awe, Jay said, "Holly! Look at the pretty jungle!"

That morning I had the good sense to walk back to my toddlers and gather two bouquets of orange black-eyed Susans and blue cornflowers and place them in outstretched little arms. Then I plucked stalk after stalk of the flat Queen Anne's lace, bending forward to point out the black, buglike middle of the flower to my appreciative children. Then I said, "When we get home, I'll show you something magic that flowers can do."

As soon as we scurried through the door, I had Jay and Holly sit at the kitchen table while I filled four large, clear glasses with water. As my children watched, I poured a few drops of green, red, blue, and yellow food coloring into separate glasses before adding the flower stalks. Even these years later, I can see those round little faces leaning on chubby little hands as we watched the blooms pull the color up into the lacy petals.

To my credit, I didn't accomplish much more that day. I just wish I'd picked a bigger bouquet. But at least

I had finally begun my journey of slowing down to enjoy my children.

An Encouraging Hug

Honey, slow down. Instead of hurrying toddlers, enjoy the world's wonders with them.

8

A Little Buddy

When I was a child, I talked like a child, I thought like a child, I reasoned like a child. When I became a man, I put childish ways behind me.

1 Corinthians 13:11

During one of Jay's college breaks, he helped me clean out an old cedar chest. As I refolded quilts, I heard Jay say quietly, "I remember him as so much bigger."

I turned to see my adult son holding a small, blue teddy bear in the palm of his hand. Ah, Blue Bear—his long-ago companion. I was looking at my tall, bearded son, but I was *seeing* a little boy clutching his buddy as together they faced a new Sunday school class, a visit to the doctor, or even a noisy car wash. Somehow the years had spun past me, and the exhausting toddler whom I had lost and chased and scolded was now all grown up. Suddenly I wanted another chance at those years. And this time I wanted to do them right. But life doesn't work that way.

Jay put the little fabric bear back into the chest and then helped me fold another quilt. And I sighed, knowing I had realized too late what I'd had in those early years.

What special moments are you sharing with your child today? All too soon they will become special memories sewn forever into your heart.

An Encouraging Hug

Honey, even when your children are grown, you occasionally will have glimpses of who they used to be.

9

Looking Ahead

Sons are a heritage from the Lord, children a reward from him.

Psalm 127:3

Since we were childless for several years, our friends had given up on the thought of our ever having a family. So when we quietly whispered the results of my recent obstetrician visit to our pastor's wife at a Sunday school party, she was so excited she waved her coffee cup in the air, forgetting it was full.

Our relatives and fellow teachers were amazed that we were starting a family, especially since they knew the intense schedules we kept. I shrugged off their all-knowing glances and comments. I was well organized, I said, and we both were such good disciplinarians in the classroom that we weren't concerned about being able to raise well-behaved children. Our lives would continue as normal, I insisted. Parenthood wouldn't slow *us* down.

The veteran parents at the school lunch table suppressed grins, but a fellow teacher, Russ, dared to enlighten me: "You don't realize it yet," he said, "but your life changed and your freedom ended the second that child was conceived."

It's a good thing it takes babies nine months to develop, because we needed all that time to absorb the changes swarming into our lives. We knew my body would change, but we hadn't counted on how much slower I would begin to move. And never had we been so aware of babies all around us—in the grocery stores, in the malls, even on the sidewalks of our townhouse complex. Suddenly our every conversation centered on our coming baby, whom we called "Little Bear." Even before seeing the child, we had fallen madly in love with him and were no longer making idle predictions that our lives would not change. And by the time Jay showed up one October morning, we were ready to have him take over our hearts.

An Encouraging Hug

Honey, my old teaching friend was right. Your life changed the moment your child was conceived. But it's a glorious change.

10

Joyful Laughter

All the days of the oppressed are wretched, but the cheerful heart has a continual feast.

Proverbs 15:15

One of my friends, whom I'll call Miranda, makes an effort each day to find something humorous to tell her children. That determination started one Sunday morning when one of her daughters said, "Mom, the other ladies laugh more than you do. Are you sad?"

The observation and resulting question startled Miranda. "Oh, I'm not sad at all," she told her daughter. "I just get preoccupied with family things."

From that moment, though, she decided to show the joy on the *outside* that she carried on the *inside*, and she began to look for ways to pull humor into her family's day. The first morning, she cooked pancakes in silly shapes and served them while wearing a clown's red nose. Throughout the day at work, she looked for amusing situations she could share with her family that evening.

"It's amazing that once I started looking for humor, I found it," she says. "The young man who delivers our office mail was juggling the padded envelopes, and I know I never would have noticed his antics if I hadn't been looking for something funny to tell my family. That evening, after my report, the kids hurried to clean up the kitchen so all of us could try juggling tennis balls. We laughed the hardest we had in a long time. And to think it all started with my little girl's comment that the other mothers were laughing more."

Perhaps you need to learn to lighten up too. As I was making this new attempt in my own life, I memorized Proverbs 17:22: "A cheerful heart is good medicine, but a crushed spirit dries up the bones," and Philippians 4:6: "Do not be anxious about anything, but in everything, by prayer and petition, with thanksgiving, present your requests to God."

If you tell God what you need—more humor in your day—he will show you all kinds of amusing situations. Now, I confess I'm still having to quote "Do not be anxious about anything" to myself even though—perhaps *because*—my children are older. A while back, preoccupied with a cousin's tense situation, I looked up the original meaning of the word *worry*. I found that it comes from *merimnao*, which means "to be distracted." And isn't that what worry is—something to distract us and keep our attention on the problem rather than on the solution? I found that when I'm worrying, I'm doubting God's ability to help. And I love it that nothing is too great or too small to talk over with him—whether we're hovering over cribs or pacing the floor on date night. Only as we talk to him will we escape the nagging, paralyzing anxiety and experience his peace.

An Encouraging Hug

Honey, worrying about the future robs you of the joy of this moment. So go ahead and trust tomorrow to the Lord and find ways to enjoy today.

11

A New Vocabulary

May the words of my mouth and the meditation of my heart be pleasing in your sight, O LORD, my Rock and my Redeemer.

Psalm 19:14

Some of the fun expressions from the days of having two toddlers in the house are still with our family in the form of coded vocabulary. Using Holly's long-ago expressions, we still call pancakes "bambakes," and hamburgers and french fries are "hangaburgers and free fries" at our gatherings. Each spring, as baby rabbits appear in the pet stores, I remember Jay as an excited toddler calling, "Daddy, take a see at the bunny rats!" And if we spy a turtle while we're on a family picnic, one of us will nudge the other and say, "Hey, there's a green sun." Both kids, though grown, know I still smile as I come across the piece of paper tucked into my Bible on which I, the nonartist, had once attempted to draw a turtle at young Jay's request. I drew the creature from a bird's-eye perspective, so the head and four little legs were jutting out from under the oval shell. Jay looked at my feeble attempt and exclaimed, "Wow! A green sun! Now draw me a turtle."

While we enjoy our fun vocabulary and the memories each word evokes, I'm reminded of the authoritative attitude one of my college professors held. She taught child development classes and let us know that speech development was serious business and proper English was to be insisted on—always. I certainly agree that the child's speech pattern development is critical, but, while it's important to help children with correct pronunciation of words, I also think parents and children should enjoy each other and enjoy each stage of development. And that includes adding new words to the family vocabulary.

An Encouraging Hug

Honey, go ahead and add a few fun expressions to your family vocabulary. The memories are worth it.

12

Peaceful Sleep

*I will lie down and sleep in peace, for you alone, O LORD,
make me dwell in safety.*

Psalm 4:8

One morning, when Jay was almost three, he came into
our room and awakened me by lifting my eyelids and
saying, "Mommy, are you in there?"

What a horrible way to be awakened! But rather than
yelling, I went to the library that afternoon for more picture books to stack at the bottom of his bed to distract
him in the mornings.

He quickly got over that annoying wake-up activity,
but *I* remembered it. One morning when he was thirteen, I was having trouble getting him up for school. So I
lifted his eyelids and asked, "Jay, are you in there?" That
night he started locking his bedroom door!

This whole business of sleep is a major issue for
families. (Doesn't it seem that for the first ten years we
try to get them into bed, then for the next ten we try to

get them out?) Here in Colorado Springs, I live near the United States Air Force Academy. As part of the grueling survivor training for future pilots, the cadets are deprived of sleep for several days. Some of our young friends have reported that the consequences can include hallucinations, disorientation, and extended weeping. Any parent who has been up night after night with an ill or fretful child can vouch for those reactions. That's why I always advise new parents to get as much sleep as possible in those early weeks, concentrating on sleep rather than worrying about the house. Getting a good night's sleep helps us face the day's challenges with brighter eyes—and greater hope.

An Encouraging Hug

Honey, sometimes the most spiritual
thing you can do is sleep.

13

Milestone Days

*How can we thank God enough for you in return for all the
joy we have in the presence of our God because of you?*

1 Thessalonians 3:9

One of my friends tells about his mother's 1930s pregnancy
in a community that didn't think a woman should be out
in public once she "started showing." Thus each Sunday
morning she would slip out of their house after service had
started at a nearby church and stand beneath the open
window to hear the singing and the sermon. As the closing
prayer was announced, she'd quietly go home.

As I shook my head at his story, he added, "But my
grandmother moved in for a while, and the neighborhood women were there for her when it was time for my
brother's delivery. They took over the cooking and all of
the housework—including the laundry," he added. "And
that was no small feat since that end of town didn't yet
have electricity."

Today we can't imagine pregnant women not being
"allowed" to be out in public. And it's sad that we can't
imagine a dozen women pitching in to take care of a new

mother. Often the extended family is too far away to be of real help, and the women of the church have jobs outside of the home, which doesn't allow them to be as available as they'd like. Today more and more young couples are coping alone. Fortunately, many young fathers are shouldering more of the responsibility too, rather than thinking childbearing is the sole responsibility of the woman. In fact I'm always pleased to hear a young wife say, *"We're pregnant,"* instead of, *"I'm pregnant."*

But even if your husband is helping, young mother, let me stress that during these early weeks, you need to concentrate on your precious baby and on your own health. And don't worry about the house.

In fact I've told more than one new mother, "Honey, don't be surprised that on some days if you brush your teeth *and* your hair before noon, it's a milestone day."

If this is her first child, she usually rolls her eyes or informs me that she certainly is more organized than that. Later when she sees me, she sheepishly confesses that I was right. One young mother even called me late one afternoon and said, "Ask me what I've accomplished today."

I chuckled. "Plenty, Honey. You took care of a helpless little being who is totally dependent on you."

So let the house get a little dusty. Let the laundry pile up. Take care of your baby and yourself. Gradually your strength will return—including your sexual strength—and your baby will settle into a routine. For now, don't try to rush all that.

An Encouraging Hug

Honey, the dusting and mopping can wait. Take care of your baby—and yourself—in those early weeks.

14

Veteran Wisdom

A cheerful look brings joy to the heart, and good news gives health to the bones.

Proverbs 15:30

Mary and Craig Stamps of Truckee, California, know the importance of incorporating laughter and creativity into their family's day. With six children ranging from toddlers to teens, that decision has proven to be a good one.

"Anything can be fun," Mary says, "but it starts with the parents' attitude and the realization that the fun leaves if you're too intense."

Even doing dishes in the Stampses' household can be fun.

"I remember the first time we asked all of the kids to do the dishes," Mary continues. "One child carried plates and bowls to the kitchen in his wagon. Another rode a scooter horse as she carried the cups. You can have fun doing anything—as long as you allow the children to use a little imagination."

A typical Stamps family activity is building blanket tents together.

"Livening up everyday activities is important," Mary says. "We read stories under tents, do homework under tents, hold family meetings under tents. Recently someone bought us a *real* tent at a garage sale that we immediately put up in the backyard. More instant fun."

"God has given us nature to nurture our spirits," Mary says. "Children—and adults—need flowers and grass and even sprouted carrot tops to look at." For those families in the city who don't have backyards where they can grow things and pitch a tent, Mary and Craig recommend potted plants—anything to give a taste of nature to the children.

Another thing the Stampses do is encourage their children to perform bunk-bed theater. "And make sure you look interested and awake while they're performing," adds Craig.

Most children like dressing up, so in the Stamps Family Theater, the children sing, dance, and tell stories while in bathrobe costumes.

"Bible stories and singing are really big in our house," says Mary. "In fact I like singing the Word of God to them at bedtime so they go to sleep with the Lord's security in their minds."

An Encouraging Hug

Honey, let your children use their imagination. Don't be bound by an attitude that says, "That isn't the right way to do it."

15

Eyeball Listening

Commit to the LORD whatever you do, and your plans will succeed.

Proverbs 16:3

Some folks are horrified that I confess my "parenting sins" so openly, but how can we encourage each other if we pretend we're perfect? Besides, I'm hoping young mothers and fathers will learn from my mistakes. Occasionally some of those parents do learn. Better yet, they let me know—as did this young mother who heard me speak at an Iowa retreat a while back. She wrote: "People think I'm a wonderful mother, but when you told the stories of yelling at your children for getting into the water or being impatient when they'd stop to look at ants, it really hit me. I constantly yelled at my kids. Every morning was a battle of trying to get out of the house on time, with me yelling, 'Come on! Get ready! You're making me late!'

"Then we'd go our different ways, and all of us would be in bad moods. I had to drive three miles to work and would hate myself the whole way. Then my day would be terrible because I had such a terrible disposition. The kids would also have a rotten time at school. But now I get them up in the morning and quietly remind them they know what is expected of them, instead of yelling and blaming them for my being late. Know what? We usually leave on time and all have a much better day.

"While I was at the retreat, both children stayed with my brother. When I returned—all ready to make a new start—my brother told me that Saturday night my nine-year-old son had awakened crying because he said I needed to get away from him and his sister. I was crushed. But that's what I had yelled earlier in the week when the two of them were fighting again in the car. I had said, 'I can't wait until this weekend so I can get away.'

"I never thought about how much that stupid remark would hurt my son. I work full time and go to school two nights a week for a nursing degree, so I would kind of wave my kids off when they talked to me. Well, the night I came home from the retreat, I sat in the kitchen and listened as my son started to tell me about what he had learned in Sunday school and how much fun he'd had. As I really listened to him, he kept inching his chair closer to me. And the more I listened, the brighter his face got. I started crying and told him I was sorry about the way things had been and that I was going to try my best not to yell at them anymore.

"The more I listened to my son, the more I realized what a smart kid I have. Before that, I hadn't known what to do with him since all he seemed to do was whine and say, 'I don't have any friends,' and 'Nobody likes me.' He'd even look at me like he hated me and wouldn't do anything I asked him to do. But now we all sit down and talk at dinner, and I don't let them take their plates to the front room to watch TV. This week we even made out the grocery list and then shopped together. Grocery shopping used to be a nightmare, but, amazingly, they were no longer asking for things that were not on our list. All I had to do was slow down and start listening to them. Thanks, Sandra."

No, thank *you* for listening.

An Encouraging Hug

Honey, children thrive on eyeball-to-eyeball listening.

16

Fun Memories

Command those who are rich in this present world not to be arrogant nor to put their hope in wealth, which is so uncertain, but to put their hope in God, who richly provides us with everything for our enjoyment.

1 Timothy 6:17

In a magazine interview, a well-known evangelist was asked what he wished his parents had done differently. He didn't hesitate: "I wish my folks had allowed us—and themselves—to have fun."

Some friends of mine have taken the idea of family fun to a new level. Sally and Frank enjoy stopping at often-overlooked places during their journeys—an obscure diner in Kansas, an abandoned cabin in Kentucky. Once, at the children's pleading, they stopped at *every* advertised museum on Route 80 as they traveled from Colorado to Illinois.

Sally says, "Believe me, the kids are going to remember that trip. We all had a great time."

When we lived in Michigan, we kept large garbage bags in our car trunk for impromptu tobogganing. Jay and Holly still mention those days of just being silly.

My sister Nancy, however, wins the prize when it comes to having fun with her daughters. Rachel and Elizabeth are ten years apart, so Nancy wanted an activity the three of them could enjoy together. She decided that clowning would fill that need and promptly enrolled them in classes. Since she's a "snappy" dresser even as a clown, she named her character Snappy and has a great time making balloon animals and cracking silly jokes. And in the midst of having fun together, they have deepened their family bond, which is one of the many benefits of laughter.

An Encouraging Hug

Honey, go ahead and laugh. That's the "grease" that
keeps a family rolling along.

17

New Taste

Then God said, "I give you every seed-bearing plant on the face of the whole earth and every tree that has fruit with seed in it. They will be yours for food."

Genesis 1:29

Recently our local grocery store offered fresh asparagus. As a young mother gathered a handful, she exclaimed to her three-year-old son, "You *love* asparagus!"

The little boy looked a little bewildered, as though trying to remember when he had last eaten those strange little green sticks, but he didn't argue.

I'm convinced his reaction would have been much different if his mother had said, "Now we're going to get some asparagus, and you're going to try at least two bites even if you don't like it."

I remember more than a couple of times when I've set my children up for a negative reaction just by my stern insistence that they give something a try—experiences as well as food. But a "Hey, let's have fun" attitude gets better results than a "This is good for you" jaw set.

When we lived in New York, the kids' school chums and my coworkers would often insist that a theater, restaurant, art gallery, or some other place just wasn't to be missed. So we made a list of all the places we—as transplanted Midwesterners—had to see. Most times we were delighted with the experience, but occasionally we'd return home, shaking our heads and wondering why our friends thought the event or place was so special. But rather than grumble about wasted time, we decided on a nonchalant attitude of "Well, that's another thing we can cross off our list." Not only did our willingness to try the unknown keep us from complaining about wasted afternoons, but it often yielded a new adventure.

An Encouraging Hug

Honey, encourage your children to accept
a new experience, whether it comes in the form
of a new dish or a new outing.

18

Encouraging Humor

A gentle answer turns away wrath, but a harsh word stirs up anger.

Proverbs 15:1

As a young mother driving her three boys to various sporting events in the Detroit area, Kay discovered her sons were less likely to pick on each other when they were stuck in traffic if she could get them to come up with wild scenarios imagining their fate. One afternoon Brian, the youngest, won when he described how they would be stuck so long that they'd be all grown-up and would grow through the roof of the car. Humor goes a long way toward lightening the moment.

Humor can work too when it's time to give the kids their chore list. Often, in our rush to assign tasks, we're tempted to say, "When you finish that, tell me and I'll let you know what you're to do next." But I've found that method to be demoralizing, since the child feels as though he or she will never be finished with work.

Instead, I used to make a list of what needed to be accomplished—often with suggested times for completion—and then had them cross off each item when it was done to my satisfaction.

I learned early, though, that sometimes nothing a parent says is going to convince kids that their parent's request is logical. Rather than pulling out the standard "because I'm the mom" command, I found a bit of humor helped whenever a grumble surfaced.

"Oh, go ahead and do what I've asked," I'd say. "And after you've finished that task, you may add it to your list of 'Rotten Things My Mom Did—or Made Me Do—When I Was a Kid.' Bring it to me, and I'll sign it and date it so you will have proper documentation for a future psychologist."

They'd huff and then go complete the work.

An Encouraging Hug

Honey, a bit of humor goes a long way in calming the situation and getting chores finished.

19

Little Acts, Big Results

A hot-tempered man stirs up dissension, but a patient man calms a quarrel.

Proverbs 15:18

Have you ever overreacted to your child's squabbles with another child?

My best caution here: Don't turn everything into a crisis.

A while back, two mothers of three-year-olds in our neighborhood got into an argument over one child squirting the other with the garden hose. The victim's mother roughly grabbed the offender by the shoulder, called him a "very bad boy," and sent him home in tears. Minutes later, the second mother stormed out of the house, yelling at the first mother.

All-out verbal war followed, with the fathers getting into it too when they arrived home from work. Within two days, both houses were on the market.

All that could have been avoided if the first mother had taken the misbehaving child home, told the second mother what had happened, and let her take it from there. Or even if the first mother did respond immaturely, the second mother could have avoided the crisis if she had reacted calmly instead of calling the other woman every bad name she could think of.

Suddenly, instead of having *two* three-year-olds, our neighborhood had *six,* judging from the actions of the four parents. And the saddest part was seeing the two little boys watch each other through the chain-link fence, longing to play together again.

An Encouraging Hug

Honey, children will squabble with playmates. Keep everyone safe, and don't get into the argument.

20

Welcoming a Different Personality

Am I now trying to win the approval of men, or of God? Or am I trying to please men? If I were still trying to please men, I would not be a servant of Christ.

Galatians 1:10

Let's be honest—all of us enjoy receiving compliments for our children's actions, performance, personality, and even looks. But our children, while they are our offspring, are not extensions of who we are. Just as we felt uncomfortable when our parents demanded we react socially in exactly the way they wanted us to, our children feel that same tension. So let's give them the freedom to be who they are rather than using them to impress others—or having them live out our childhood fantasies.

For Rebecca, an outgoing type who loves giving parties with lots of guests, it took work to accept her daughter's shyness and preference for quiet outings with only one special friend. But she was willing to make the attempt because she wanted to create an atmosphere that would encourage her child to be who God created her to be.

A tough question we occasionally may have to ask ourselves is this: Can we handle the delightful challenge of the individual, or are we more comfortable with impressing our friends with our ability to produce the perfect child? If perfection is our goal, we're in for a disappointment.

But once we relax and enjoy our children for who they are—and for what their interests are—rather than who we want them to be, a new depth comes into the relationship.

I had to learn that lesson, as usual, the hard way. When I was growing up, two older cousins received bride dolls for Christmas one year. The beautiful dresses, pearl earrings, and dainty, painted fingernails fascinated me, but I never told anyone how much I wanted to have my very own bride doll. Instead, I just determined that someday I would have a little girl and I would buy her the prettiest, biggest bride doll available.

Of course I had to wait a few years, but finally I got my daughter. As I watched how five-year-old Holly took care of her baby dolls, I decided the time had come for my fantasy to be realized. So I took her to the most exclusive doll shop in our area. The shelves were filled with beautiful creatures—colonial dolls with their long cloaks trimmed in fur, Victorian dolls with their hair piled high and wearing long dresses with lace collars, and bride dolls. Oh, the assortment of bride dolls! So I steered my wide-eyed daughter toward that particular case.

"Pick any doll, Holly," I said. "I'll buy any one you want."

She looked at the bride dolls for a moment, then at the Victorian dolls. Finally, she turned to me and said, "Do I have to get one of these, Mama?"

Astonished, I said, "You mean you don't want one of these dolls? But they're beautiful."

"No," she said. "I want one of those." And she pointed to a basket filled with three-dollar plastic baby dolls. So I grumpily bought her the doll she wanted, deciding perhaps she was too young to appreciate the exquisite bride dolls.

The next year, we were back at the same shop, and I was making the same command: "Pick any doll you want."

Again six-year-old Holly shunned the beautiful dolls for another blue-blanketed plastic baby doll. Again I decided she was just too young. This scenario continued for the next three years. Finally, the nine-year-old Holly, now wise to my antics, looked at the dolls, then looked at me with solemn eyes and said, "Why don't you buy a bride doll for yourself, Mom?" Sigh. Good point.

One of my friends, Missy Poppinger, recently sent me a miniature Madam Alexander bride doll with a note: "Here's your bride doll. I don't ever want to hear that pitiful story again!" Of course I appreciate her loving gift, but I'm not about to let go of my fantasy. One of these days maybe I'll have a granddaughter . . .

An Encouraging Hug

Honey, God in his vast creativity made all of us different.
Let's enjoy that difference.

21

The Dinner Hour

Better a meal of vegetables where there is love than a fat-tened calf with hatred.

Proverbs 15:17

When both of my children lived at home, we had a house-guest for several weeks. At our first dinner together, she offered to help me put the drinks on the table. I handed her a glass of apple juice and asked her to put it at Jay's place, pointing to the chair near the window.

She looked astonished, then asked, "Do you guys have assigned seats?" I answered, "Well, no, they're not really assigned seats, but we always sit at the same spot."

She shook her head, "I've never heard of such a thing. At my house, we just fill our plates and sit wherever we want at the table."

Since I grew up in a family in which everyone had his or her own seat at the table and then later presided over such a table in my own home, I hadn't thought anyone would find habitual seating unusual. But the important thing is not where you sit but that your family eats together.

Kati read an article that said children in families who don't eat together are more prone to delinquency. She showed it to her husband, Brad, and they decided they were going to stop this business of lining up at the microwave before rushing off to Little League and tennis lessons. At first, they managed to eat only one weekday evening meal together, but now they're up to three nights a week of sitting down together. Not only are they eating healthier meals, but they're amazed that having dinner together has added a new closeness to their family—and a new calmness.

An Encouraging Hug

Honey, make it a habit to have dinner together—no matter where you sit.

22

Tangible Care

Rejoice with those who rejoice; mourn with those who mourn.

Romans 12:15

For years, our family verse was Romans 12:15, which provides good direction for harmony. After we chose it for our verse, I met a number of families who had chosen it for theirs too.

So how can it be applied? Well, when the eight-year-old excitedly runs in to say he made the soccer team, no sneering is allowed from the twelve-year-old. And when the sixteen-year-old is crying because she wasn't chosen for the debate team, no one is to say, "Oh, that's no big deal. You'll get over it." Sharing the rejoicing and the mourning helps us all live in harmony.

And, of course, that harmony begins with listening to each other. Often, in order to do that, we have to turn off the TV and talk. It's important to analyze TV-watching time. Are those shows just time-stealing stuff?

Parents get frustrated that the kids don't want to talk but then keep the television on. What if you turned off the TV and made a game out of asking questions that can't be answered with a yes or no, such as, "What was the best thing that happened to you today?" or "What is the worst part of the day for you?"

When fourteen-year-old Jerry answered that the worst part of his day was lunch, his parents heard for the first time about the hazing of the freshmen in the lunchroom. Alerting the administration to the need for adult supervision took care of the problem and helped Jerry relax so he could concentrate on his class work. Amazing things happen when we take the time to listen to our children.

An Encouraging Hug

Honey, your children look to you to set a tone of harmony.

23

A Morning Blessing

I pray for them. I am not praying for the world, but for those you have given me, for they are yours.

John 17:9

Ever notice that when we're already running late on school mornings, that's when somebody wants a permission slip signed, needs a bag lunch for the field trip, or can't find the overdue library book? On those mornings, the last thing we want to do—but the very thing that we need to do—is take a deep breath and pray.

Even on their most rushed mornings, Marcy and George make it a practice to pray a blessing over each of their three sons before they leave for school. With their hands on each boy's head, one of the parents will pray something such as, "Lord, thank you for Davy. Thank you that you will be with him today as he takes the science test and that you will help him remember those things he has studied."

At first, the boys squirmed under their parents' hands, but soon they began looking forward to the prayers, even reminding them, "Hey, we gotta pray!" when they are running especially late. Today those three little boys are tall teens, but they still wait for their morning blessing before they head out the door to drive themselves to school. Not only has that morning prayer affected these three young men, but the memory and the practice undoubtedly will be passed on to their children as well.

An Encouraging Hug

Honey, energize your mornings with a prayer of blessing.

24

Simple Reminders

I thank my God every time I remember you.

Philippians 1:3

Recently Cal and his wife were going through some boxes from the back of a closet. As his wife checked the contents of one yellowed envelope, she pulled out several small, folded notes.

"What are these?" she asked.

Cal opened one and then smiled, "Oh, these are the notes Mom used to put in my lunches."

Then, caught in a tender moment, he tossed them back into the box saying, "Hey, be glad I didn't keep the banana skins. When she was in a hurry, she'd write encouraging notes on the fruit."

Ah, I used to do that too, sometimes even drawing faces of guys with big ears and frizzy hair.

I'm not surprised Cal kept the notes all those years. What his mother had thought would be just a simple little thinking-of-you note had proven to be an important encouragement.

While even something as simple as a note tucked into your child's lunch says "I'm thinking of you," occasionally try to have lunch with your child. Recently fifth-grader Joseph called his mother at her office to ask if she could bring a hamburger over to his lunchroom that day. Her morning schedule was light, so she agreed to meet him in the cafeteria hallway. To her amazement, as he thanked her, he said if she wanted to stay and talk, it would be okay. She did exactly that. The next week, he asked if maybe she could bring him another hamburger on Tuesday. She caught on that time. And she's been treasuring their Tuesdays together, knowing that next year, when he goes into middle school, he'll be too "cool" to be seen eating with his mom.

An Encouraging Hug

Honey, include your children in your workday.

25

Scary Moments

*You will keep in perfect peace him whose mind is steadfast,
because he trusts in you.*

Isaiah 26:3

A few years ago, when I was senior editor for a family magazine, I had the fun of interviewing Diane, the mother of four active children. As we talked about scary moments in parenting, she told the following experience.

"I will never forget the first time I left our four children home by themselves. I needed to run to the store for milk and diapers, so I told Sarah, then twelve, and her younger brothers, Gary and Daniel, to be good and let the baby, Spencer, continue his nap. I knew I'd be gone no more than twenty minutes.

"But when I returned home, I drove up to every parent's nightmare—two fire trucks in the driveway, an ambulance on the front lawn, and two police cars at the curb.

"The blood drained from my face as I struggled to catch my breath. Why had I been so foolish as to leave them alone? How was I going to tell Tim I'd killed our children?

"I jumped out of my car and ran toward the house, sobbing. Just as I started up the drive, a husky policeman grabbed me in a bear hug and wouldn't let go, even though I was struggling.

"Just then, Sarah, Gary, and Daniel came running out of the house, sobbing.

"'What happened to the baby?' I wailed.

"'Nothing,' Sarah managed. 'He's still asleep.'

"Bewildered, I looked from child to child and realized they were crying only because I was. Then the policeman directed my attention to a downed electrical wire near the driveway. He hadn't been trying to keep me from going into the house—just away from the dangerous wire that had fallen while I was gone. A neighbor had spotted it and called the electrical company, who in turn sent all the emergency equipment. With my knees still trembling, I took the three children back into the house. I didn't leave them home alone for a long time after that.

"In fact it was a year and a half before I had the courage to leave the children alone again. On that particular day, I'd been especially busy with laundry, preparations for that night's church supper, and answering letters. Spencer, twenty months old by then, was stacking his blocks on the family room carpet while Daniel, eight, read nearby. It was a perfect time to mail my letters at the corner mailbox before the five o'clock pickup.

"I explained to Daniel I would be back in just a couple of minutes and that he was to watch his little brother's every move.

"I practically ran the half block, threw the letters into the mailbox, and hurried home. But as I opened the door, I was greeted by a frantic Daniel.

"'Mom, I'm so sorry,' he sobbed. 'I didn't mean for it to happen. I took my eyes off Spencer for just a moment . . .'

"I gasped, 'Oh, no!' and rushed past Daniel, expecting to find Spencer sprawled on the floor, dead.

"Instead he was standing by the kitchen table with chocolate brownie smeared all over his face. He was enjoying the dessert I'd prepared for the church supper."

Poor Diane. In that moment, she undoubtedly decided she could never leave the children alone again—ever. At least not until they were married.

An Encouraging Hug

Honey, it takes only a moment for bad things to happen when young children are left alone.

26

Home Alone

*Do not forsake wisdom, and she will protect you; love her,
and she will watch over you.*

Proverbs 4:6

Knowing when to leave children home alone is often
a major decision for parents. When my husband, Don,
died of cancer in 1982, I found myself faced with the
challenge of raising a ten-year-old son and eight-year-old
daughter by myself. I soon learned that for parents (and
single parents in particular), this issue of leaving the
kids—even for quick errands—is especially difficult.

All across America, the time between the hours the
kids come in from school and the parents get home from
work can be especially nerve-racking. One of my friends
paid an older neighbor to go into her house each afternoon and start dinner for the family just as the children
arrived home from school. Since the woman supposedly
was helping their mother, the children didn't think of
her as a baby-sitter.

Other parents I know have hired a college student to assist the children with homework after school. I especially like this idea since it takes some of the pressure off the parents to supervise the lessons when they get in from work. Another couple arranged to have their preteen daughter help at their church's day-care facility. The girl was able to spend time with the toddlers—an age group she enjoyed—and the parents knew she was safe.

And while you're taking those precautions, make sure you set up rules—that the kids help shape—to cover chores and visitors. In our home we had a simple rule—no visitors if I wasn't home. Later, when they were in their late teens, that rule was occasionally bent when they were studying for exams with a classmate, but only if the visitor was of the same gender and the other parent knew I wasn't home.

An Encouraging Hug

Honey, prayer, planning, and family discussion will help you come to a good solution.

27

A Favorite Photo

We have different gifts, according to the grace given us.

Romans 12:6

Oh, sure, even with good humor, it's often difficult to get through this business of being a family. With a little bit of thought and lots of prayer, though, we can do exactly that. I hope it's encouraging for you to know my family has come a long way since our early intense days. In fact my favorite family photo—taken the day before Jay left for college—captured the essence of who the three of us are—and it was the one the photographer snapped as a practice shot. He kept telling us to back up, even though we were approaching the edge of a cliff at a local park.

As my heel caught on the edge of a large crack in the rock, I called out, "Hey, I'm going to fall here," and started to laugh at the ridiculousness of the situation. Jay immediately put his elbow on my shoulder and said, "Relax, Mom," as Holly, in her usual embarrassment over the antics of her goofy mother and nonchalant brother, leaned toward us and sternly whispered, "You guys!"

From all of the shots the photographer offered us, the practice shot is the one I chose to have on my dresser.

So which family photo best captures your family dynamics? I hope it's one in which you're all laughing.

Remember Russ, my friend who announced that life is never the same after a child is conceived? He was right, of course, but I wouldn't trade this chaos for the world!

An Encouraging Hug

Honey, have fun displaying those less-than-perfect family photos.

28

A "Cookie Baker," Anyone?

Two are better than one, because they have a good return for their work: If one falls down, his friend can help him up. But pity the man who falls and has no one to help him up!

Ecclesiastes 4:9–10

The last time we moved, Holly and Jay were sixteen and soon-to-be eighteen. I knew they were capable of staying at home by themselves when I had to leave town for a few days at a time on business, but still I worried. And I hated the thought of their coming home from school to an empty house every afternoon. So remembering my friends who'd had an older neighbor start dinner each day just as the children arrived home, I offered to have a "cookie baker" occasionally come in. Jay saw through that right away.

"Mom, look at us. We're too old for baby-sitters. Besides, with the situation heating up in the Middle East, I may get called into the military. And if the government thinks

I'm old enough to fight for our country, surely I'm old enough to protect my sister for the few days you'll be gone each month."

Hmm. Well said, Jay. But I was still nervous about those nights he would be late getting home from play practice, so I ordered a security system from a reputable company. Cliff Stoker, the owner/installer for American Bell Security, came highly recommended by a close friend. As we discussed the various safety features of the system, I confided my concern about leaving Holly. I didn't think much about the conversation again until a month or so later when I returned from yet another trip. Holly had an interesting report for me. She had set off the alarm by accident and promptly called the monitoring center to report the mistake. As soon as Holly hung up the phone, it rang.

"Holly, this is Cliff Stoker from the alarm center," the caller said. "Just answer yes or no. Is anyone there with you who shouldn't be?"

She was touched by his concern. "Oh, no, Mr. Stoker. I'm here alone and I really did set off the alarm by accident."

His sigh of relief came through the phone. "Well, good. But make sure you call us if you have any problem at all."

That simple call made us all feel even more secure. Oh, a few folks scolded me for getting a security system, saying I should trust the Lord. I do, but I learned a long time ago that he expects us to add common sense to that trust.

An Encouraging Hug

Honey, the peace of mind that comes with a good security system is worth the cost.

29

Add Some Joy

Rejoice in the Lord always. I will say it again: Rejoice!

Philippians 4:4

Our attitude toward each other sets the tone for the home. And that attitude starts with basic respect for each other. Remember, negative attitudes are contagious, and the parent's outlook on life truly affects the child. On Chuck Swindoll's radio broadcast a couple of years ago, he told a joke to explain the difference between a pessimist and an optimist. The optimist had a hunting dog he was really proud of, so he often bragged about him. One day the pessimist said, "You mean that old hound you've got in your backyard? He doesn't look so special to me."

The optimist then suggested they go hunting so he could show this man what a fine dog this truly was. As they went, the pessimist grumbled the entire time about the weather. As soon as they arrived at the duck blind, a flock flew over, and the optimist shot two ducks in rapid succession. He then called for his dog to retrieve the fowl, and the dog joyfully took off. But instead of jumping into the water and swimming to the ducks, the dog walked on top of the water! He retrieved the ducks and turned to walk back on top of the water to his master. The optimist stood there grinning and said, "What do you think about that?" The pessimist shrugged. "He can't swim, can he?"

Kind of makes you wonder what he would be like as a parent, huh? When folks like that come into a room, it makes you turn around and ask, "Who turned out the lights?"

A joyful attitude is so much better. Now, somebody out there just grumbled, "What do I have to be joyful about?" Remember Philippians 4:4? For many years I read it as *"Rejoice in the Lord always. I will say it again: Rejoice"* (emphasis mine). Somehow I thought that meant I had to be happy about everything. But the verse doesn't say, "Rejoice *always*." It says, "Rejoice *in the Lord always*." We don't necessarily rejoice in circumstances, but we rejoice in the Lord. So even in the midst of difficult times, we can say, *Thank you, Lord, for being with us in this situation. Thank you, Lord, that you will bring your good out of this.* What a difference that makes!

An Encouraging Hug

Honey, no matter what life hands us, we can still rejoice in the Lord.

30

Read to Your Babies

They read from the Book of the Law of God, making it
clear and giving the meaning so that the people could
understand what was being read.

Nehemiah 8:8

Educators tell us that children who are read to even
before they can understand the words score higher on
intelligence tests than do other children. I know of more
than one parent who has read to the baby even before
the child was born. That was always going a little too
far for me, but I agree it's good to establish positive
habits early.

I read to my children while I nursed them, even in
the middle of the night. I confess my motivation wasn't
always pure, since many times I was reading aloud just
to keep myself awake. But the babies were hearing my
voice and picking up the rhythm of the words. I read
aloud the Bible, James Michener novels, and even the
classics, including the translation of the Norse *Volsunga*

Saga, on which Tolkien based much of his imagery. Once, when I was especially tired, I tried softly singing some hymns from my childhood, but that made me all the more relaxed and sleepy. So on such nights, I just recited nursery rhymes but saved "This little piggy went to market" for counting toes at diaper changings.

Occasionally some church friends scold me for having recited nursery rhymes, pointing out their original political meanings. But, like it or not, nursery rhymes are part of our literary culture, and allusions to those rhymes show up all around us. In fact, as my children began to read on their own, I introduced them to the Greek and Roman influence on our culture as well. Yes, I would point out a beautiful sunset or delicate flower and comment on God's creation, but I also mentioned such things as our morning cereal getting its name from Ceres, the Roman goddess of grain. For teens, this can lead to a discussion of the culture during the time of Jesus and can provide an even greater appreciation for Paul's message on Mars Hill. I'm convinced wonderful ideas await your child through books.

An Encouraging Hug

Honey, enjoy reading to your babies. Both of you will enjoy the special cuddling time—and the intellectual results are real.

31

Special Company

Do not forget to entertain strangers, for by so doing some people have entertained angels without knowing it.

Hebrews 13:2

Ever notice that we always manage to get the house picked up and a good meal on the table when we're expecting special company? As a church family, we take to heart Hebrews 13:2, apparently believing that displaying gracious hospitality toward others is the eleventh commandment. But what if we occasionally treated our family in that same way? I remember a husband in our long-ago Sunday school class who confessed that one afternoon he took a long look at the messy condition of the living room and kitchen and said, "I think it's about time we had some friends over after evening service Sunday"—knowing he and his wife would work together to get everything in shape.

As his listeners chuckled and nodded, Bea said she noticed the cleaning that took her forever was accomplished in less time—and with the family's help—when company was expected. So one Saturday morning, she confided a plan to her husband, Jack, then excitedly told their four children, who ranged in age from six to twelve, that very special guests were coming in just a few hours. She handed each one a list of chores to be completed in record time, including bathroom cleaning and yard work supervised by her husband, and charged into her own chores, which included vacuuming, polishing furniture, preparing a tasty pot roast, and baking a cake, which she decorated with the words "For Our Favorite Company."

By midafternoon, the work was finished and everyone was bathed and dressed in company clothes. After Bea smiled her approval, Jack instructed the children to go around to the front and ring the bell. They looked a little bewildered but did as asked. Then Bea and Jack opened the door and welcomed their "special guests" with smiles and hugs! And the children loved it.

An Encouraging Hug

Honey, have fun treating your family like special company occasionally.

32

What Do You Want?

Blessed is the man who finds wisdom, the man who gains understanding.

Proverbs 3:13

One of my friends, whom I'll call Clara, says for years her mother didn't know what would make her happy, so her mother wanted everything. That meant that all during Clara's childhood, each Saturday was a long day at the mall, hunting for just the right outfit or new pair of shoes. Many times the item went into the closet with the tag still on it and remained there for weeks and even months. Obviously her mother did not need the item for a specific event but had purchased it in an attempt to fill an imaginary hole in her heart.

Perhaps you know someone like this as well who says shopping makes her feel better. And when she goes out, she expects to come home with several purchases.

St. Augustine said there's a God-shaped void in our heart nothing but God can fill. No number of purchases, no number of antiques, no collection of jewelry or even fine art can fill the hole. So how do we change those bad habits? As usual, change starts with becoming aware of the problem, then praying about it and being open to the solutions—including new attitudes—that come out of those prayers.

For Clara's mother, it took the suggestion that she help during Clara's volunteer shift at a women's shelter. As her mother saw women who had run from their homes and abusive relationships barefoot, having time to grab only the baby, her emotional world began to expand.

Shortly thereafter she cleaned out her closets, taking many of the clothes with the original tags on them to the shelter. As she found a way to feel useful, she no longer needed to fill her life with meaningless activities and the accompanying accumulation of things.

So take a look around. Are you filling your life and the lives of your family with clutter? Find ways to reach out to others and enrich your days.

An Encouraging Hug

Honey, your children notice when you enjoy filling your life with people—not things.

33

Heaven Is Not Here

*There is no one like the God of Jeshurun, who rides on
the heavens to help you and on the clouds in his majesty.
The eternal God is your refuge, and underneath are the
everlasting arms.*

Deuteronomy 33:26–27

For years I was a slow learner when it came to perfection. Somehow I got it into my head that if I worked
hard enough and looked long enough, I would find the
perfect job situated in the perfect locale. I knew heaven
wasn't in Kentucky, since my family had been forced
to be part of the 1950s Great Migration due to the lack
of jobs. I quickly had learned from our northern community's dislike of Appalachians that heaven wasn't in
Michigan either.

Then three years after my husband died, I was offered
an editorial job with a ministry an hour north of New
York City. I prayed earnestly and was determined not to
go unless the Lord was the one inviting us. But while I

wanted only the Lord's leading, I also was convinced a ministry would provide the perfect setting in which to serve the Lord. Thus I moved my two young teens and our mellow cat to New York. Those four years in the East were interesting, challenging, and even fun—and none of us would trade the adventure—but we quickly learned heaven was not there.

Next came the invitation to Colorado Springs, the mecca of evangelical Christendom. Again the Lord was leading, so we moved. To my amazement, heaven isn't in Colorado either.

Did we miss the Lord's leading with these moves? Not at all. He had opportunities for me to minister in each location, and he had things I needed to learn—including that heaven is only in heaven. I finally have that lesson secured in my head. So in case you're still looking, let me spare you a great deal of wondering—and wandering—heaven is not here, not any place on this earth. Yes, keep praying about that possible move and be ready to go when he calls you, but don't go expecting everything will be perfect.

Now, what does that insight have to do with parenting? Plenty, because your actions and choices today affect your children's future. After all, if you are convinced the *next* move or the *next* job will be perfect, you will be disappointed. Remember, among his many promises, the Lord offers his peace (John 16:33a), his power (Acts 1:8), his presence (Exod. 33:14), his purpose (Rom. 8:28; Eph. 3:11), and *trouble* (John 16:33b). I could have done without the promise of trouble, but at least we know what to expect.

So while disappointments undoubtedly will come, we can meet them in the Lord's strength. And as your children watch your reactions, their ability to set their own realistic expectations will be strengthened.

An Encouraging Hug

Honey, while no place is perfect, each place still has
much to offer. Have fun exploring—and appreciating—
your locale.

34

Take Charge

*Do not work for food that spoils, but for food that endures
to eternal life, which the Son of Man will give you.*

John 6:27

Experts have differing opinions about mothers working
outside the home while the children are small, so I'll
add my opinion to the mix. Pray a bunch, ask yourself
if you need to work, and then decide what's best for
your situation.

By the way, this work stress is not just a phenomenon
of this era. During World War II, women built the air-
planes their men flew. More than a few of my Detroit-
area friends tell about being taken to Grandma's to sleep
so their mothers could work in the Willow Run war
factory. In fact Carrie's grandmother kept a pile of quilts
in the corner of the living room where her five grandchildren slept curled up against each other like puppies
until their mothers came in from midnight shifts.

When the men came home from the war, they took over the jobs. And from 1946 until the early 1960s, the women, for the most part, went back to the kitchen (and bedroom) and started producing the babies who became the great Baby Boom. Today women are working outside of the home again and in ever increasing numbers. So how are we juggling all our responsibilities?

In an undated news clipping from our local paper, I read, "Instead of waiting for corporate America to get the message, working mothers are taking the lead by starting home-based businesses, providing contract labor, and sorting out other flexible work arrangements that allow them to adjust their hours to their children's needs."

Notice the key phrase in the previous sentence: "Working mothers are taking the lead." It's up to us to know what we need and then figure out a way to meet the need that will benefit both our situation and our boss. Some companies have caught on to "flex" time, allowing parents to set working hours so they can pick up their children, attend a school meeting, or take a child to the doctor. But traditional companies haven't adopted this concept yet. I know more than one large company that insists their workers work an eight-to-five shift—with mandatory and unpaid overtime tossed in.

Some parents alternate their shifts so one is always available to be with the children. For example, Tim works as a security guard from 6 A.M. until 2 P.M. He then stays with the children while his wife, Lori, leaves for her job at a nearby nursing home, where she works from 3:30 P.M. until midnight.

"Sure, it's tough," Lori says, "but we've chosen to do this so our children will be raised by us—not somebody watching twelve other children."

This whole business of child care has to be the greatest problem for the young working family. I remember those days, and I'm glad to be finished with them. But I have plenty of regrets too and hope you and your spouse are talking about what will work best for your family. This isn't an isolated problem either. The Bureau of Labor Statistics says that today more than half of mothers with children under age three work. So you are not alone in your decision if you go back to work after the babies arrive. Just remember, pray like crazy, check out the caregiver's references, watch how your child reacts to the caregiver, occasionally stop in unexpectedly, and trust your instincts.

An Encouraging Hug

Honey, remember to pray a bunch about this decision.

35

Memory Stones

I remember the days of long ago; I meditate on all your works and consider what your hands have done.

Psalm 143:5

On my stove shelf is a jar of pebbles that has traveled from Michigan to New York to Colorado Springs with us. My guests wonder why I display so proudly a jar of rocks, but those are the stones that then- five-year-old Jay and four-year-old Holly handed me throughout our first day at our new summer place on Lake Michigan. While my husband, Don, and I cleaned and unpacked, Jay and Holly spent the day jumping off the low deck into the sand, pausing every few jumps to find a pretty pebble to show us. We'd exclaim over each one, give the kids a hug or two, and then drop the stone into a glass pint jar. Even now, those pebbles bring back happy memories. When I'm an old woman in the rest home, I hope I'm allowed to keep that jar with me.

One of my artist friends, whose paintings of Rocky Mountain cabins appear in Denver galleries, remembers the 1970s smiley face she painted for her grandmother years ago. Last year, when she helped her mother clean out her grandmother's house, the smiley face was still prominently displayed in the bedroom. What a little girl had seen as just a fad painting had been treasured by the grandmother who had not only loved her but encouraged her to follow her dream to be an artist.

An Encouraging Hug

Honey, go ahead and display that special item—and don't worry what your guests think.

36

Creating Good Memories

If you, then, though you are evil, know how to give good gifts to your children, how much more will your Father in heaven give good gifts to those who ask him!

Matthew 7:11

My grown children don't remember expensive toys or my perfectionistic housekeeping, but they do remember the midnight we impulsively donned snowsuits over our pajamas to make angels in the new snow on the front lawn. And those are the types of things your children will remember too.

If you need some ideas, here are a few simple things that anyone can do:

Get excited about the bugs. Mary Stamps remembers her little ones calling, "Mom! Mom! I need you to see this bug!"

With six children, it would have been easy for her to think she couldn't be torn from the task at hand, but she says, "By taking that minute to look at the bug, my child felt nurtured for the rest of the day. Otherwise, he felt neglected." She continues, "I won too, because I saw a bug I wouldn't otherwise have seen. Parents need to see these times as God calling us to take a break, to come away with him for a moment, to get refreshed, and then to go back to our work."

Keep the camera handy. When Mary's four-year-old, Josh, received a bubble-making kit as a birthday gift, the other children showed him how to make giant bubbles. Soon they pulled her outside to see the bubbles too.

She says, "Sometimes the beauty around us is in our children, so I started taking pictures of their faces as they watched Josh's delight." Those bubble photos are now some of the family favorites.

Explore your neighborhood. Children don't need to go to fancy theme parks to have a great time. Take walks around your block and give them the assignment of pointing out at least two things they hadn't seen before. On our walks, we liked noticing how many different shades of green we could find. Our record is fourteen.

We occasionally visited our nearby fire station where the men would let the kiddies climb up into the front seat of the truck. As a thank-you, I always took along a plate of brownies.

Record your adventures. Sometimes I jotted a note on our family calendar, but usually we made cassette tapes of our adventures to send to the grandparents. Those tapes are now treasures.

Go to the park. My toddlers loved feeding the ducks at the local pond, so I usually kept a supply of stale bread in the car trunk for any unexpected bird sightings. At one pond, though, we got a surprise as we tossed the bread to the swans and saw the water churn before the birds could grab even one morsel. The pond was packed with fish! What fun to hear two little kids—and one excited mother—squeal over the sight.

Consider the child's interest. While you're looking for fun things, don't lose track of the child's perception of fun. One of my favorite *Family Circus* cartoons shows the family at the zoo—with all four children on their hands and knees studying the ants on the sidewalk.

An Encouraging Hug

Honey, pleasant memories are a far better gift than anything you can buy.

37

Encouraging Chitchat

*Listen, my son, and be wise, and keep your heart on the
right path.*

Proverbs 23:19

The teen years can be frustrating when our normally
talkative children suddenly clam up. Of course, we can
try asking questions at dinner that cannot be answered
with just a yes or no—"What was the most frustrating
thing that happened today?" or "What was the most
interesting thing you did in chemistry class?" But even
those questions may not provide much information,
especially if your son is like mine, who responds to "Tell
me about your day" with one word: "Forgettable." So
we have to find a place where they *will* talk.

For us it was in the car when we went for drives. Jay
was usually quiet at home, so when I noticed he would
talk in the car, I began scheduling long Sunday tours
of our New York countryside. Holly happily napped in

the backseat, providing Jay and me with special "alone time."

In fact I enjoyed those talks so much that when his year at an Ohio college ended, I flew out and rented a car, and we drove to our new Colorado home together. Of course, he was perfectly capable of putting his luggage on a plane and getting to the Rocky Mountains by himself, but I wanted those twenty-three hours of conversation. And what a treat that proved to be! I heard the details of what had been only brief phone reports, and I had an opportunity to encourage him.

Oh, in case you're wondering about my daughter, I seldom had to ask about her day. She was ready with the information as soon as she came through the back door. For my friend Marty, though, her children were just the opposite. Her son was always willing to give details of his favorite classes, the food fights at lunch, and who got "busted" for wandering the halls without a pass. To get her daughter to talk, Marty invited her for a walk each evening. She said it was amazing that as twilight descended, her quiet daughter would begin to open up, expressing concern about everything from pimples to peer pressure. Those moments of connection gave Marty the opportunity to help her daughter stay on the right path. And isn't that what all of us parents want?

An Encouraging Hug

Honey, find a place where your child is comfortable talking.

38

Opening Your Home

*Let love and faithfulness never leave you; bind them around
your neck, write them on the tablet of your heart.*

Proverbs 3:3

Years ago, a neighbor of my in-laws installed thick, white
carpet in her living room and then promptly secured a
blue ribbon across the doorway to keep her teens and
their friends out. I can understand wanting to keep things
nice, but somehow that gesture hit me wrong. Apparently
it hit her teens wrong too, because they started hanging
out at their friends' houses instead of in their own home.
And the sad thing is the mother was glad she didn't have
to put up with their noise and clutter.

When Don and I heard this, we decided our home
would always be open to our children and their friends.
So on summer afternoons, we had a backyard full of
kids loudly throwing water balloons or dodging Mr.
Wiggle, the sprinkler toy. As our children became teens,
water puddles on the floor were traded for pizza stains

and soda pop spills on the carpet. Still, homes are supposed to be places people live in, not tiptoe through. Besides, whenever my teens entertained their friends in our home, I knew where they were and what they were doing—important involvement that did not go unnoticed.

In fact one Christmas break, as I sat at the kitchen table writing checks for bills, Jay came through the front door with four of his friends behind him and called to me, "Hi, Mom." As I answered, "Hi, honey," each of his buddies echoed the same "Hi, Mom," which I answered with "Hi, honey." The last one through the door, Derek, grinned and said, "Don't you just love it when we're all home?" Ah, I truly do.

An Encouraging Hug

Honey, yes, it's time-consuming and sometimes inconvenient to have a houseful of young people, but it's, oh, so important.

39

More Warm Welcomes

Let your conversation be always full of grace, seasoned with salt, so that you may know how to answer every-one.

Colossians 4:6

Are your children's friends welcome in your home? Do they sense an attitude that says, "I accept you"? Yes, we are to watch for disreputable influences, but we also can provide an acceptance that will open the way for us to later share our faith.

When Jay was in college, he dated a young woman whom he teasingly called "Earth Muffin." I enjoyed meeting her, of course, and we chatted pleasantly about her studies and her job. Later, when Jay and I were alone, he turned to me.

"Isn't she great?" he asked.

I nodded. "She really is sweet, Jay. I can see why you enjoy spending time with her." Then I grinned wickedly.

"But please remember I never batted an eye when I saw her nose ring."

Jay's eyes widened. "Wow, that's right. She does have a nose ring. It's such a part of her, I don't even notice it." I think I gained yet another measure of respect in his eyes for not making a big deal out of her facial jewelry. And the young woman didn't feel defensive each time she was in my presence.

That same year Jay and another friend, "Shoe," drove to eastern Oklahoma to visit some friends. They figured they had a fifteen-hour drive ahead of them, so I packed one of my typical travel lunches: five roast beef sandwiches for each, apples, grapes, snack crackers and cheese, soft drinks, and brownies with Kentucky black walnuts. Amazed, Shoe watched everything go into the insulated bag and commented that when he had decided to take time off from work (and his paycheck!) to visit friends, all he had received from his folks was a terse "You'd better be able to make your car payment."

After I hugged Jay good-bye, I asked Shoe if I could give him a hug too. He grinned and then gave me a bone-crushing hug that made me wonder how often he—and other shy kids like him—get hugged.

An Encouraging Hug

Honey, you have a mission field right in your own home
as your children's friends sense your open heart.

40

Start When They're Small

As for God, his way is perfect; the word of the LORD is flaw-less. He is a shield for all who take refuge in him.

2 Samuel 22:31

While Mary Stamps has learned to enjoy spontaneous "bug appreciation" adventures, she and her husband, Craig, also know that with six children they must have basic goals to accomplish each morning. Thus they have what they call "finger chores"—chores done with little hands that must be taken care of first thing every morning. Those activities include praying, getting dressed—complete with socks and shoes, the importance of which is clear to anyone who has ever tried to find the second shoe just as you're ready to go out the door—making the bed, picking up dirty clothes, and then having breakfast. After that, each child must do a family chore, such as washing the dishes.

"Children need organization," Mary says. "If everyone does his or her chores, you can keep things orderly. But once those basic chores are complete, you must be open to the unexpected."

Being open to the unexpected can include talking about God in a new way.

"One morning I read in the Old Testament how the priests had called all the people together to hear the Word of God," Mary says. "So I took the kids outside, put a blanket on the ground, and said, "We're calling a solemn assembly to talk about the things of God."

Then she proceeded to talk about the kind of music they should listen to, how to know if their clothes please God, and what God says about their appetites.

"We talked about the subtle things that please God," Mary says. "They all heard, and I was amazed at their understanding—even at their young ages."

So just as we teach our children to do simple chores early, we can be confident they are never too young to absorb the Word of God.

An Encouraging Hug

Honey, teachable moments are all around you. Be open to them.

41

A Missed Opportunity

This is the day the LORD has made; let us rejoice and be glad in it.

Psalm 118:24

Housework, laundry, cooking, and concerns about the workplace will always be with us, but the moment of sharing something special with our child may not.

But even knowing that, I still tossed away a marvelous opportunity to share a special moment with my daughter several years ago. We were living in New York, and I was on the phone with my new Colorado boss as we worked on a difficult story. We took a couple of short breaks, but I didn't take a break at the most important time—when Holly saw a rainbow and called for me to join her outside.

I will always regret that I didn't excuse myself from the phone and join her in time to see one of nature's spectacular events. On my early morning walk the next day, regret overwhelmed me, and I did ask the Lord to give me another chance—and another rainbow to share with Holly.

But that chance didn't come until almost a year later and long after we had moved to Colorado. This time I was ready and dashed outside at her first squeal of "A double rainbow! Ya gotta see this!" I grabbed the camera on the way out, and Jay took our picture as Holly and I stood together with the rainbows over us.

But we parents have no guarantees of that second chance. So let's grab all those rainbow viewings—and similar adventures—each time they appear. Remember, the work projects will always be there, but the rainbows—and our children—won't.

An Encouraging Hug

Honey, the world can wait while you grab
rainbow moments.

42

Stinging Words

*Set a guard over my mouth, O LORD; keep watch over the
door of my lips.*

Psalm 141:3

Margie's relatives always send her the old photos they
find when they're cleaning closets. As the unofficial family historian, she's usually able to identify the subject
and supply information about the event and the year.
Recently, as she sorted through a shoe box full of black-
and-white photos her cousin had sent, she was startled
to find one of herself in her late teens. To anyone else, it
was simply a forty-year-old picture of a young girl standing on a porch, looking away from the camera. But in an
instant, she remembered the day her aunt had snapped
the photo of her in a new dress. Her smile in the photo
was forced, and even four decades later she remembers
that just as her aunt said, "Oh, Margie, honey, you look
so pretty," her dad, drinking beer in the shade, snorted

and said, "Hey, Sis, didn't you say you have to get new glasses this week?"

Margie remembers she didn't wear the new dress much after that; it always brought back the painful scene and reminded her she wasn't as pretty as her older sister, whom her dad called "Princess."

Margie, today, is finishing her master's degree and is well respected within her profession. But in an instant, as she looked at the old photo, she was that young girl again, feeling the sting of her father's words—and the accompanying mocking rejection. Our words as parents have greater power than we think, so let's choose them carefully.

An Encouraging Hug

Honey, we can undo some of our own childhood hurts by passing on encouraging words to our children.

43

Old Tapes

Like a madman shooting firebrands or deadly arrows is a man who deceives his neighbor and says, "I was only joking!"

Proverbs 26:18–19

Karen—like many other adults—understands pain-filled memories. To this day she remembers asking her father what he thought of her Easter outfit. His retort was a stinging "You'd be pretty if you'd put a bag over your head!"

At her hurt look, he had laughed and said, "Hey, can't you take a joke?"

But to Karen, it was no joke. If her own father thought she was ugly, then she truly must be.

Further, she brought home *A*s in English, but her father wanted a mathematician. On looking at each report card, he'd say, "When you bring home *A*s in math and science, then you'll be somebody." The translation, of course, was that right now she was nobody.

Another friend, a man who commands great respect within the academic community, carries those internal parental barbs as well. Even though his intelligence earned him a postgraduate degree, he refuses to do even the simplest handyman job around the house. Why? Because during my friend's childhood, his mechanically talented father berated him each time he tried to help, laughingly introducing him as "Mr. Fumble Fingers" to neighbors.

I know only too well that the need for acceptance doesn't end when we leave childhood. In 1988 I had just finished interviewing Sarah Cannon—known to the world as Minnie Pearl—when she invited me, along with Jay and Holly, to sit in the seats behind her on the Grand Ole' Opry stage as she did her comic routine.

Years before, a relative had dismissed my conference speaking with a shrug, saying, "If you're ever on the Grand Ole' Opry stage, then you'll be somebody."

So sitting behind my favorite comic, I confess I couldn't wait to get back to our hotel to call the relative and let him know I had, indeed, just gotten off *that* stage. But as I gave the details during the call, he grumbled that he had meant if I ever performed there.

"Well, you never said I had to perform," I teased.

Remembering my own struggles, I once interrupted the writing of an article on acceptance—and Jay's reading of the evening paper—to ask if I had encouraged him lately.

"Oh, sure, Mom," he answered. "You didn't bug me when I changed my major in college. I appreciated that." Having said that, he then added, "Guys don't need encouragement the same way girls do. You women encourage us when you let us read the paper in peace."

Oh. End of discussion.

An Encouraging Hug

Honey, the words we parents plant within our children's hearts carry the power to encourage or to defeat.

44

The Hippopotamus

May your unfailing love be my comfort, according to your promise to your servant.

Psalm 119:76

When Jay was two, we moved into a new house where he seemed to adjust quickly—until it was time for bed. Then, uncharacteristically, he would cry, saying he wanted to go to his old house. I tried to reason with him, saying we had a *new* house now. But his pleas of "Not new house, *old* house!" troubled me for three nights.

Then one morning, as I continued to unpack our belongings, I found the oversized poster of a purple hippopotamus reading a book that had been on the wall near his bed since birth. Suddenly I realized that he didn't miss the house; he missed the poster that he thought we had left behind. Immediately I hung the poster by his bed in the new room and then took him by the hand to see it. His smile let me know I had correctly guessed the source of his unhappiness. (By the way, Jay kept the poster in his room through two more moves. In true teen fashion, he just tacked it to the ceiling.) Often our children don't have all of the information they need. In this case, Jay was too young to comprehend the idea of packing and unpacking; he just knew he missed his poster. And while I made sure he had his favorite stuffed animal, I never thought he had grown that attached to the purple hippopotamus. That event helped me not assume that children know what's going on.

Some of my older friends say they learned their children needed more information about a lost job that forced one parent to be away searching for a new job. If the child is very young, we have to do a lot of guessing while we are providing extra comfort in the form of hugs and our physical presence. For an older child, we may have to take extra time to explain the situation. But no matter the age of the child, we can't assume he or she has the information needed.

An Encouraging Hug

Honey, sometimes you have to hear beyond the words to know what is going on in that little mind.

45

Immediate Action

*Fathers, do not embitter your children, or they will become
discouraged.*

Colossians 3:21

I had a boss once who seldom talked to his department
members about a situation when it occurred. Instead,
we had to face the event several months later when
he'd open his file on us at our review. Thus, instead of
learning immediately from our mistakes, we were dis-
heartened as we watched him pull a scrap of paper out
of his file and tell us something "bad" we'd done three
months earlier. That doesn't work in the office, and it
certainly doesn't work in the home.

Just as my coworkers and I would have appreciated
immediate and private correction, our children need the
same direction. If our children don't know that they have
been rude or thoughtless in a situation, this is the time
to help them see that others have feelings too. Give a
gentle explanation such as, "Jenny was very hurt when

you made that remark about her outfit. How do you think you would have felt if someone had made that type of comment about what you are wearing today?"

One of our friends was frustrated at a Little League baseball game when, by the second inning, his son was pulled out of the pitching spot, but instead of chiding his son for his lack of ability, he asked some very gentle questions: "What do you think would help you improve? Would you like me to catch some of your pitches for the next few weeks when I get home from work?"

Yes, all of this takes extra time, but the payoff is much better than it would be if we just hauled out that file, whether it's emotional or physical, three or four months from now.

An Encouraging Hug

Honey, confront—and solve—problems immediately.

46

Phone Hugs

A word aptly spoken is like apples of gold in settings of silver.

Proverbs 25:11

Just because teens act tough doesn't mean they no longer need us. In fact I remember Sam Levinston, a teacher turned comic, who used to say, "Little children, little problems. Big children, big problems."

For a while, our teens may pull away, but a time will come when they gladly accept reminders of our love and perseverance—even when they're away from home. It's fun to give a long-distance hug over the phone. As Holly signed off after calling from college, I'd always ask, "Are you ready for a hug?"

At her usual "Am I ever!" I'd say, "Okay, close your eyes. Imagine I'm putting my left arm at your waist. Now my right arm is going across your shoulder. Ready?"

At her affirmative answer, I'd say, "I'm pulling you close. Now smushing you."

Then I would make grunting sounds, often until I was breathless, according to her mood—light grunts if it had been a good week, long, deep grunts if she was working through a problem. By the time I'd finished, we both would be laughing at the ridiculous sounds, but she would be reminded she is loved.

An Encouraging Hug

Honey, teens need us too. Find ways to let them know you care.

47

Little Ears

Our mouths were filled with laughter, our tongues with songs of joy.

Psalm 126:2

In 1906 the mother of one of my now elderly friends died, leaving three small children for her husband to care for. He couldn't do it alone, so they all moved in with his widowed mother. Once, in front of the oldest child, a friend at church commented to the woman about her taking in her grandchildren. She dismissed the compliment, saying gruffly, "Well, one has to do her duty."

Even as an adult, the granddaughter often mused, "I wish we had been something other than a duty."

True, wouldn't it have been wonderful for them to have been a *joy*? But my friend confesses the scene is painful when she remembers it only through the eyes of a child.

Today, with an adult's understanding, she knows how difficult it was for her grandmother to have her serene days interrupted to care for three young children after she had already raised her own five. Her grandmother was elderly and still grieving the death of her beloved daughter-in-law. But even with the adult's understanding, she still wishes her grandmother had had the energy to put her arm around her and say, "I hope you know how much I love you." But then she thinks about her stern grandmother and knows such a response was beyond her ability. She realizes sadly that laughter and "songs of joy" were not part of her grandmother's personality.

An Encouraging Hug

Honey, be careful of what you say in the presence
of your children.

48

Early Lessons

Unless the LORD builds the house, its builders labor in vain. Unless the LORD watches over the city, the watchmen stand guard in vain.

Psalm 127:1

Karen's father showed up at her wedding rehearsal drunk, as usual, and then proceeded to show off his supposed wit with inappropriate remarks. Before the wedding party left for dinner that night, Karen's mother matter-of-factly suggested she call her uncle to ask him to stand by in his best suit the next day, just in case her father was too drunk to attend the wedding. It never occurred to them that such planning wasn't normal! Her family had gotten so used to making secondary arrangements around her father, Karen thought that was the way life is.

To Karen's amazement, her dad did manage to stay sober long enough to walk her down the aisle, but she entered marriage with one well-grounded thought:

Always have a backup plan. Obviously she and her husband had some big emotional hurdles to climb over during their first few years of marriage.

Children who have grown up in families that don't quite work right (I'm weary of the overused word *dysfunctional*) seem to live by three rules: *Don't talk, don't trust,* and *don't feel.* And those characteristics affect the adult the child becomes. But I offer that principle merely as an explanation, not an excuse, because I'm also weary of adults who refuse to accept responsibility in life, preferring to be a victim and blame their parents for everything bad that has happened. While it's important to look at these issues and learn from them, it's also important to grab the Lord's hand and move forward. The sad thing is that many of their early experiences still affect adults today, keeping them from accepting the many good gifts our Lord wants to give.

An Encouraging Hug

Honey, you don't have to repeat your parents' mistakes.

49

Solid Direction

You have made known to me the path of life; you will fill me with joy in your presence, with eternal pleasures at your right hand.

Psalm 16:11

The visiting missionary held his little girl's hand as they waited for his wife in the foyer of our Michigan church. Various folks stopped to welcome him to the missionary conference, but one man scowled at him. Instead of saying hello, he flipped the visitor's tie and said, "Kind of fancy for a missionary, isn't it?"

That grumpy man's young son was watching. Is it any wonder the little boy later, in Sunday school class, told the missionary's daughter she couldn't play with the *new* game?

We have heard that our values are more *caught* than *taught*. While we nod our heads and give lip service to that, we sometimes forget its truth in practice. But before we can put our values in front of our children, we have to decide what they are.

As you're thinking about what specifics you want your children to learn from you, you might think about a scene from the book *Alice in Wonderland*. Remember when Alice asks the Cheshire Cat which way she ought to go?

"That depends a good deal on where you want to get to," said the Cat.

"I don't much care where—," said Alice.

"Then it doesn't matter which way you go," said the Cat.

And that's just the way it is for parents. Before we can decide how to get our children on the right path, we have to know where we want to take them. Do you want your children to be kind, generous, watchful for God's touch each day? Then you have to lead the way on the path you want them to follow.

An Encouraging Hug

Honey, you're not just raising a child; you're shaping a life.

50

Good Examples

The LORD detests men of perverse heart but he delights in those whose ways are blameless.

Proverbs 11:20

Margaret's son and ten-year-old grandson were with her the Saturday morning she switched price tags on a sweater at their local department store.

Her son protested, "Mom, that's wrong. Besides, it's not a very good example to set for Ryan."

She merely shrugged. "Oh, come on. You know that sweater is way overpriced."

Three years later, Ryan was arrested for shoplifting and had to go to court. The court clerk was Margaret's neighbor and saw her in the hallway. "I'm so sorry, Margaret," she said. "I know it's difficult for you to have to be here because of Ryan."

Margaret nodded. "I just don't understand why he would do that. He's certainly been taught better."

Hardly.

Now, I'm not saying our bad examples will result in jail sentences for our children or grandchildren, but we do have influence over our children's actions. Let's strive to make sure our example is encouraging them to be the young men and women God is calling them to be.

One of my friends said the only thing that kept her out of an inappropriate sexual relationship was the thought of one of her sons meeting the overnight guest in the hallway the next morning. Yep, we can't expect our kids to make good moral choices if we refuse to make them ourselves. And none of this saying "It's different for us" since we're adults. One single mother challenged me on that point, saying she had been married before, so what did she have to protect?

"Respect," I answered, "your children's as well as your own."

It's amazing how powerful our spoken instructions can be as well. For example, since honesty was very important to my parents, they began early to pass that quality along to their children. My mother would finish her admonishments with "Be a woman of your word" and then follow up her words with her own godly example. My dad would tell us that honorable men and women don't lie, proving it in his own life. But in typical no-nonsense style, he always added a practical reason to the moral lesson: "The truth is easiest remembered."

Those seemingly little examples carry great weight.

An Encouraging Hug

Honey, as we make good moral choices, our children will be more prone to do so too.

51

Not Wrong, Just Different

The man who eats everything must not look down on
him who does not, and the man who does not eat every-
thing must not condemn the man who does, for God has
accepted him.

Romans 14:3

One thing I have tried to teach Jay and Holly is that the
entire world doesn't have to do things the same way we
do. One of those lessons included showing them there's
room for many different styles of worship. So when we
lived in New York, we once drove forty minutes south
to attend a church of a different denomination, where
we'd heard the Word was powerfully preached.

Jay liked the church the moment he saw the drums in
the orchestra section. That excitement was carried over
into the sermon, which was full of promise for those who
love the Lord and full of threat for those who have yet to
make their peace with him. Then the altar call was given,
and eight or nine people made their way to the front of

the church. Just as the minister started to deliver the closing prayer, the copastor, his wife, stepped forward. "There's still somebody who needs to get right with God," she said. "He's calling you. I don't understand this, but the word *orange* means something important to you. So you get down here *now!*"

Suddenly, from opposite ends of the sanctuary, two men were out of their seats like shots and almost ran to the altar. We three were starting to lose brain cells over what we had just witnessed. As Presbyterians we settle our sins with God immediately and in the privacy of our hearts, so this was new to Jay and Holly.

Then before the pastor prayed, he suddenly pointed toward the upper rows to our right and said, "Mother, your son is coming home!" A woman in that direction shrieked with joy while another woman standing at the altar and directly beneath his pointing finger keeled over with a sickening thud—stone-cold out.

The three of us dropped our jaws, but nobody else seemed troubled. One of the women sitting in the front row brought a red cloth and draped it, for modesty, over the fallen woman's legs while the minister kept talking. At that point, he did gesture toward the woman and say, "Don't worry about her; she's all right." Sure enough, at the close of the prayer, the lady who had dropped the cloth over the fallen woman's legs helped her up and walked into the counseling room with her.

We couldn't wait to get home to ask a Pentecostal friend about what we had seen. He said the phenomenon of someone keeling over used to be called "slain in the Spirit" but that the new term is "resting in the Spirit." He assured me it doesn't hurt.

So as I passed along the information to Jay and Holly, I tried to stress that God reaches people in different ways—just as his Son healed people in different ways. I reminded them that sometimes he spoke (as in Matt.

9:6). Sometimes he healed based on the faith of another (as in Matt. 8:13). Sometimes he touched (as in Matt. 8:3, 15; 9:29). And at least once he made a mud paste from spittle which, when put on the blind man's eyes, caused him to see (as in John 9:6).

That one service provided opportunities for several evenings of intriguing dinner conversation.

An Encouraging Hug

Honey, if God can work in many different ways, who are we to expect him to do things only our way?

52

Forgiveness

Do not judge, and you will not be judged. Do not condemn,
and you will not be condemned. Forgive, and you will be
forgiven.

Luke 6:37

Forgiveness is one of the toughest areas for us as parents to teach our children. We know the truth of Luke
6:37, but many of us still have events stuck in our craw
from years ago. We may even tell ourselves that when
we refuse to forgive, we are not only keeping ourselves
from God's blessing, but we are letting that other person
live "rent free" in our head. And we know the one who
wronged us is not losing sleep—we are. Even secular
counselors say getting rid of grudges is good for us. We
know all of that and still our stomach tightens each time
we think of a particular person. And it's only worse when
someone has hurt our child.

I remember when I worked in New York as an editor. A
young mother had written to ask advice from one of our

regular contributors. She told how, in a fit of anger, her husband had backhanded their six-year-old daughter, resulting in the blinding of the child's left eye. As she poured out her heart in the letter, she said her husband was repentant, that he had attended anger management classes, and that each day he was trying to be the husband and father he knew he should be. But, she went on, she still felt deep resentment toward him each time she looked at their daughter's blind eye. Then she asked, "How do I deal with this?"

The columnist had answered in a way I thought was too flippant as he merely said, "You have to forgive him." I sent his answer back asking for more detail. He then expanded it to include that forgiveness *is* a process but it is only when we are able, by God's help, to let that person off the hook and not demand he pay for this act for the rest of his life that we will finally be free from the constant gnawing of our spirit. That helped, but still I was troubled over the situation.

Then, a few years later, one of my friends was angry with me, so she was exceedingly rude to Holly when she stopped in to see her daughter. Holly came home, hurt and bewildered, but since I didn't have the concept yet of what forgiveness truly means, I told her to just stay out of the woman's way and let the rude comments go. Holly was able to do that, but I couldn't. I wish I had been like Hannah in 1 Samuel 1:15 when she was wrongly accused by Eli of being drunk. She could have responded by slinking out of the temple, wringing her hands, and saying in self-pity, "Oh, Lord, nobody understands." Or she could have responded by yelling at Eli and saying he was a foolish old man who did not know the situation. Instead, she chose the more respectable part and said, "Not so, my Lord," and explained the burden of her heart. Because of her gentle exclamation, Eli asked God to grant her petition.

I should have called my friend and gently asked for an explanation. Instead, I let my feelings fester for more than a year, while my friend forgot about what had happened. Obviously our friendship suffered in the meantime.

I wish I had known my friend Dr. Linda Williams's definition of forgiveness: "Forgiveness is the willingness to live with the consequences of another person's sin." So, then, forgiveness is a decision of even the reluctant will.

These are lessons we parents must settle within our own spirit before we can pass them on to our children.

An Encouraging Hug

Honey, the willingness—making the choice—to live with the consequences of another person's sin can be freeing.

53

Consider the Child

Train a child in the way he should go, and when he is old he will not turn from it.

Proverbs 22:6

Parents are fond of quoting Proverbs 22:6 to each other, often to remind a mother or dad concerned over a wayward teen that the story isn't over. That Scripture is encouraging indeed. But some Bible scholars interpret the first part of the verse as "train a child in *his* way." That is, take the individual child's personality into account when applying instruction and discipline. After a recent conversation, I rather like that understanding.

During a chat with Dave, a buyer for a major circus based in Florida, our conversation turned to my favorite animal, the elephant. Soon Dave commented that even the best trainer can't *make* a multi-ton elephant do anything, then proceeded to explain how the performance is based on mutual respect. The trainers study the animals before they begin training them, watching for those things that a particular creature enjoys doing.

Thus, if an elephant likes rolling things with its trunk, he will be the one chosen to roll the gigantic ball around the ring. If a young lion rolls over a lot, the trainer will have him do that on command in the act. If a horse doesn't flinch when he's near the tiger cage, he will be trained to carry the tiger on his back.

I was fascinated with that insight. What if we applied this concept to our children? What if we knew our offspring so well that instead of demanding they do things our way, we allowed them to function in their own natural areas of giftedness?

An Encouraging Hug

Honey, trust your instincts when it comes to your children. You know best their potential and their limitations.

54

Wise Choices

For you have been my hope, O Sovereign LORD, my confidence since my youth.

Psalm 71:5

I'm at the age at which I finally understand the old saying "Youth is wasted on the young." But still, the only thing I miss about those long-ago days is my smooth skin! I wouldn't want to go through all that again—unless I could go through it knowing what I know *now*. Of course that's impossible, so my next best option is to encourage young people that the best years are still ahead—if they don't mess them up by making stupid choices now.

"So why do our parents say these are the best?" one of my Michigan high school students once asked.

I threw the question back to the class. The answers ranged from "lack of responsibility" (most of the other students hooted at that), "good figures" (*I* nodded at that one), and "choices." If nothing else came from our discussion, the students had an opportunity to be encouraged, to see life from their parents' perspective, and to name some of the stupid choices they could make—taking drugs, indulging in premarital sex, getting in trouble with the law, just to name a few. But not one of them ever said they were having the time of their lives right then.

Today I live across the street from a high school, and I'm amazed at the number of slump-shouldered students who walk past my drive. These are young people who are beautiful and strong and, I'm assuming, don't have to think about how their bodies move when they jump over the high curb or vault the wooden fence that leads to a shortcut through the neighborhood. Few, if any, look as though they're having the time of their life. As I watch them, I pray for them—trusting they are able to make the good choices now to protect the coming better years.

An Encouraging Hug

Honey, remind your teens these are not the best years of their lives.

55

Creative Strength

Be strong and take heart, all you who hope in the LORD.

Psalm 31:24

Does your family have a Plan B for those times when your first choice doesn't work out? During Jay's and Holly's teen years, we joked that we had so many things go wrong, we also had to have plans C, D, E, F, and sometimes triple Z. But I wanted to teach them, as the old saying goes, "There's more than one way to skin a cat."

I have a pair of three-inch carved work shoes on my office shelf that remind me not to give up when immediate plans don't work out. The carver, a Kentucky mountain man named Fred, made several of those shoes perfectly. Once, though, while working on the top of one, he cut too deeply—and out snapped a piece of the wood. He started to throw the damaged shoe into the fireplace but looked at it again with new eyes. Picking up the broken piece, he whittled a little mouse to set inside—just as though the creature had eaten away part of the shoe. Then, with a grin, he put a higher price tag on the item.

Not only did I want my children to have that kind of creative perseverance, but I wanted them to think ahead. Thus, even in young childhood, they pondered questions on our walks, such as "What would you do if a man stopped in a car and said he wanted you to help find his puppy?"

As they got older, my questions were a little more complicated, such as "What would you do if one of your friends wanted to copy your homework?"

In their early teen years, as I was concerned about the pressures they would encounter from their peer group, I asked questions like "What would you do if one of your friends offered you a joint or some interesting looking pills at a party?" I also told them that until they had enough strength of their own to say no, they were welcome to borrow mine. Thus I suggested they reply, "Are you kidding? I can't do that; my mom would kill me. And you've seen her. She's a big woman. You know she can do it."

Of course they'd chuckle, but a preplanned answer gave them an escape if they needed it.

Occasionally they also used my strength to help them turn down invitations to places they didn't really want to go. More than once, I would hear them say during a phone conversation, "Oh, no, I can't go there. My mom would have a fit."

Our children need creative strength for the challenges life will toss their way. And it's up to us as loving parents to help them develop it.

An Encouraging Hug

Honey, your children need to borrow your strength until they can muster their own.

56

Telling Stories

*These commandments that I give you today are to be upon
your hearts. Impress them on your children. Talk about
them when you sit at home and when you walk along the
road, when you lie down and when you get up.*

Deuteronomy 6:6–7

My Kentucky grandfather had a way of making the
Scriptures come alive as he retold the stories of those
long-ago people and their challenges. But along with his
retelling the biblical accounts, he also told stories of our
family. And one was as real as the other to me.

Do your children know their family history? Do they
know who you were before you became Mommy and
Daddy? Do they know what your childhood holiday
celebrations were like? Children love stories—about
how their parents met, their own birth, and the antics
of aunts and uncles. My life has been enriched by the
stories my relatives loved telling, so I looked for ways
to get our children excited about hearing some of those

same stories. Their favorite method was a stack of three-by-five cards on which I had written such statements as "Ask Daddy to tell a story about being in the same class as his cousin Tommy." Or "Ask Mommy to tell about her puppy Blacko." Each night at supper, I'd place a different card under each child's plate, which they could read as soon as they had finished eating. All of us looked forward to that part of the meal.

One evening our dear elderly friend Doris Schumacher was visiting, so the cards asked for specifics about her childhood. When she described her early 1900s Christmas, all of us felt as though we were in the parlor with her.

"The tree—with real candles on its branches—was the center of our celebration," she said. "But we children didn't see it until Christmas morning. Our tree was set in real moss and surrounded by a little picket fence Grandpa had brought from Germany. Inside the fence was a wooden Noah's ark, complete with hand-carved animals. In the corners of the fence were bowls of goldfish.

"Even though the tree decorations never varied from year to year, my brother, sister, and I squirmed through breakfast and hurried through the dishes, anxious to see the wonders beyond the parlor door.

"Our gifts were simple; practically nothing was ever purchased," she continued. "We usually started making things in October for each other. One year, Grandma and I made hand-stitched handkerchiefs trimmed with tatted lace. We crocheted a lot back then, including lacy corset covers. One year I received *The Youth's Companion*, a children's magazine, from a rich aunt. From my father, the village blacksmith, I usually received shoes.

"The tree stayed up for a week, until just after New Year's Day. We burned the candles for only a few minutes each evening, but that was the highlight of the year as we watched the tiny flames and then carefully blew them out a little later.

"Our holiday lacked the frantic stress it seems to have today. It was a time for relatives—those who could stand one another," she said with a twinkle in her eye—"to gather, to tell stories, and to eat the special German foods Grandma had spent days preparing on her wood-burning stove."

By this point, both children were bursting with questions and asked Doris to explain tatted lace and what a blacksmith did and what corsets were. Even these years later, I still remember Doris's delightful laughter at the children's reaction to her description of a corset. And all that came because we made a game out of storytelling.

An Encouraging Hug

Honey, find fun ways to pass along family stories
to your children.

57

More Stories

I will open my mouth in parables, I will utter hidden things, things from of old—what we have heard and known, what our fathers have told us.

Psalm 78:2–3

If you aren't sure about your ability to tell a story, look to Jesus as your example. Think about the stories the Son of God often told. He grabbed his listeners' attention by presenting situations with which they would identify, using examples from their daily life.

And it's never too early to start telling stories to your children. My extended family is filled with Kentucky storytellers, so as a child, I fell asleep to the sounds of the adults in the next room talking. And don't worry if your teens aren't interested. They may go through a time when they don't want to hear what it was like when their parents were younger, but when they get older and see the greater picture of family connectedness, that desire to hear stories often returns.

Don't think you have to be professional, either, by adding dramatic voices and hand gestures. Just talk normally to your child about some of the things that happened to you or your relatives. My stories usually start with the signal "That reminds me of the time when . . ."

Here are a few other suggestions:

Keep it simple. Consider the age of your child as you choose your stories. Little ones especially like hearing about their own early years and accounts of when you were their age as well.

Tell stories that bring up bigger issues and encourage discussion. When Jay and Holly began dating, I had plenty of zany stories to tell about my own teen experiences. They laughed as they pictured me trying to throw gutter balls on my first nonchurch date with their dad—only to have them hook and turn into strikes, which resulted in my beating their competitive father. That quickly prompted a discussion of the old rules that mandated women pretend to be weak.

Be prepared to repeat favorites. Children love repetition—especially if it involves one of their earlier activities. So don't scoff if your child repeatedly asks you to tell about his first birthday party when the dog jumped up to lick the frosting from his face.

Don't tell partial stories. If you don't want to tell a family secret, don't even hint at it. I had to learn that lesson the hard way. One evening, we three were at our favorite restaurant when Jay asked about a situation I'd once mentioned. I shook my head.

He looked at Holly, then grinned. "Mom, if you don't tell us," he said, "we're going to sing 'Happy Birthday' to you very loudly until you do."

I laughed. "You guys can't threaten your mother. If I don't want to tell you those details, I won't. Besides, it's not my birthday."

He nodded at his sister, and immediately they started singing at the top of their lungs. Everyone in the restaurant turned and smiled at the sight (and sound!) of two teens singing to a very embarrassed mother.

"Come on, you two," I said.

They stopped. "Are you ready to tell?" Jay asked.

I shook my head. "This is blackmail. You don't do that."

So they started singing again. Finally I could do nothing but tell them what they wanted to know. What would you have done?

Tell stories of God's faithfulness, even in the "little things." Sometimes children see God more clearly when they hear about the ways he provides for our daily needs. Tell them about the times in your life when God has shown you that he cares even about the "little things." Our children need to hear the stories from us that no one else can tell.

An Encouraging Hug

Honey, you have a wealth of stories in you that will bless your children.

58

God's Provision

Cast all your anxiety on him because he cares for you.

1 Peter 5:7

One morning during my childhood, I thought my mother was talking to herself as she looked in our kitchen cabinets. But as I listened closely, I realized she was asking the Lord for a dollar. I heard her tell him why she needed it, and then she thanked him for the way he would provide. A few minutes later she went outside to get the mail and discovered the wind holding a dollar bill against the porch, right under the mailbox.

I've often pondered my mother's prayer—and others like it—especially at those times when God has chosen to say no to one of my requests. Oh, I wish that every morning the doorbell would ring and when I answered, there would stand God.

"Good morning, Sandra," I'd like him to say. "This is what I plan to do today for you and your family. Is that all right?"

Now, I know his ways are perfect. I just wish he were open to suggestions.

But one thing I have learned is that God is still present even when we can't see him. Here in Colorado Springs, we see majestic Pikes Peak most days in our high-desert climate. But occasionally clouds obscure the sight of that magnificent 14,100 feet of granite. On those days we here in the city don't throw our hands up, grumbling, "I knew it was too good to be true! We moved our family here to be closer to Pikes Peak, but it's gone!"

No, we know the peak is there—even on the days we can't see it. And in that same way, we can teach our children God is still with us even when we can't feel his presence and he isn't answering our prayers the way we'd like.

It's like Jay gently said to his sister once when she was wondering yet again why their dad had died when they were so young: "Holly, God is God, and we're not."

That's a good reminder no matter how he has chosen to answer our prayers.

An Encouraging Hug

Honey, keep encouraging your children to pray in specific ways and trust him to answer in his time and in his way.

59

Children's Prayers

Is any one of you in trouble? He should pray. Is anyone happy? Let him sing songs of praise.

James 5:13

Jesus commended children for their faith and trust, saying we adults should be more like them.

I learned that power in the midst of a Michigan storm as I was driving home from taking then-three-year-old Jay and his little sister to the doctor. Both of them had been running fevers, so I was anxious to get home, but the pelting rain made our trip dangerously slow. Suddenly our car lost power, and I had to pull hard on the wheel to get us safely to the side of the road. Stunned, I didn't know what to do. I sat there watching the rain pour over the windshield as though someone were aiming a fire hose at our car.

I tried starting the car, but it made a strange grinding sound. I turned the key again. Still no power. I looked out at the heavy rain. I couldn't take sick children out into that torrent to walk the half mile home. I turned the key again. Nothing. Now what?

Jay broke the silence as he started to cry. "I wanna go home," he wailed.

I felt like crying too, but I said, "Jay, don't cry. *Pray.*" So with his little voice quivering, he said, "Dear God, please help us."

I added the "Amen!" and then turned the key again. This time the engine backfired several times but finally caught.

"Keep praying, Jay," I called as the car limped the several blocks home to the safety of the garage. Breathing my own prayer of thanks, I put both children to bed and then waited for Don to come home.

When I told him about our trouble and Jay's prayers, he shook his head. "The car can't be that bad or you wouldn't have been able to drive it home," he said gently. "It'll be fine tomorrow."

The next morning, he couldn't get the engine to turn over even once. After he called the tow truck, I merely said, "I'm telling you—Jay's prayers got us home last night."

This time Don nodded.

An Encouraging Hug

Honey, remind your children of their part
in God's miracles.

60

Tangible Reminders

Splendor and majesty are before him; strength and joy in his dwelling place.

1 Chronicles 16:27

Does your home reflect who you are? What special items do you have in your kitchen, living room, workshop? Do your children know the stories behind those articles? Nearly everything in my home holds a story—the 1903 chair made by my great-grandfather and his son, my beloved Papa Farley; the blue dish my great-aunt Mollie gave me the day she told long-held family secrets; the quilts made from feed sack material that cover my office walls; an antique button jar to remind me life is more interesting when we're not all perfect pearl buttons; and the little framed circus pony I embroidered with wobbly stitches when I was five. But my favorite treasure is a slightly rusted Bunny Bread sign from an ancient general store near my grandparents' home in Harlan County, Kentucky. Bunny Bread was baked there years ago, and as a child, I learned to watch for those bread signs as indicators we were getting close to my grandparents' house.

What stories are connected to your possessions? Missy loves telling the story about receiving a photo of one of her great-aunts. The frame around the picture was ornate—perfect for the wall in the master bedroom, so Missy put it there. But apparently the spinster aunt didn't like hanging in a married couple's bedroom, because the photo fell off the wall three times before Missy finally gave up and placed the photo downstairs in the dining room. It never fell again.

An Encouraging Hug

Honey, look around your home and enjoy telling the significance of each special item.

61

Passing the Baton

Better a little with righteousness than much gain with injustice.

Proverbs 16:8

What stories do you hope your children will someday be telling *their* children? Here's one, I trust, that will become part of our family history. It is the account of one of the leanest—and best—Christmases my children and I ever celebrated.

In 1990 we moved from New York to Colorado Springs. I thought our New York dwelling was sold, but as we drove across the country to our new home, the Gulf War crisis was heating up, the East Coast economy was collapsing, and the potential buyer backed out. We arrived in the West to the news that I was the not-so-proud owner of two dwellings. There was nothing to do but pray and tighten our financial belts.

A few weeks before Christmas, I had to use the last of our savings to pay the bills, which included both mortgages. But I thanked the Lord we still had thirty-four dollars left in the checking account.

So with Christmas looming, we had to get creative. I still wanted—and needed—new friends to come over for Christmas dinner. But we were going to have to rethink our plans for gift giving. Thus, three weeks before Christmas and over one of my inexpensive pasta dinners, I explained our financial crunch. My friends—also single parents—were relieved at my suggestion we exchange homemade items or gifts of service. We also agreed we'd see this as an adventure rather than "belt tightening."

Christmas morning arrived under incredible Colorado blue skies! Our family time began with our own early morning gift exchange. Not having money forced the kids to come up with creative, inexpensive gifts. These are ideas I hope they'll carry over into their future. Jay gave Holly tickets for math help, and Holly promised to do several loads of his laundry. Jay's gift to me was a sheet of coupons for eight long walks together. Holly's gift was a free-verse poem called "Parenting," in which she thanked me for being a "great person and mom." Of course I cried when I read it. After all, many parents don't have things like that said about them until they're dead.

A few hours later, the other families arrived for dinner. Each brought a special dish, creating a bountiful table. When it was time to open gifts, we exchanged plates of homemade cookies, promises to help each other with errands, and creative gifts, including spray-painted avocado candlesticks. It was an incredible day—and all because we were determined not to let lack of money spoil our fun.

The New York place was finally sold the spring after our arrival in Colorado, and we were, once again, able to keep Sears and J.C. Penney in business. Amazingly, though, it is that Christmas of 1990 to which we refer when we share fun memories from the past. What could have been a depressing time has become a story of faith to pass on—and the standard by which we measure family fun. Years from now, I'm convinced, Jay and Holly will be telling their own children about the year "Grandma Aldrich" got down to thirty-four dollars. Stories are a remarkable Christmas present to pass along to the next generation.

An Encouraging Hug

Honey, lean times can provide special blessings.

62

Typical Arguments

*Let us therefore make every effort to do what leads to peace
and to mutual edification.*

Romans 14:19

Allison called the other evening to give a report about
her new work status. She wasn't even into the third
paragraph of the conversation before she had to excuse
herself.

I could hear her in the background talking to her
teens: "Hey, you two, I'm on long distance here. Could
you please settle that a little quieter?"

When she came back to the phone, she said, "I thought
they'd be over that by now. I swear they argue every time
I get on the phone."

I grinned, of course, remembering those times when
I'd pick up the phone and it seemed as though my little
ones would look at each other and, without a word,
communicate, "Mom's on the phone. What can we do?
I know; let's *fight.*"

Yep. Kids can't help it. They appear to be programmed to do exactly that.

One young mother keeps special games and coloring books near the phone that the children are allowed to play with only when the phone rings. When she hands those out, she knows she has just bought herself about half an hour of peace.

And speaking of children's arguments, I once thought children would never argue if their parents were doing a good job (seen in my naive attitude of *"Our* children will never do that!"). But I've learned they'll always find something to disagree over.

Once, fourteen-year-old Holly looked at Jay's disaster area of a room and said, "Jay, how can you live like this?"

He took her by the elbow and gently steered her back to her pristine, everything-in-its-place room. "Holly, how can you live like *this?*" he asked. "They could operate in here!"

I had two rules when they arrived at their disagreeing (and disagreeable) stage. Rule One: No battles, either physical or verbal. Rule Two: You don't have to like each other, but you do have to respect each other.

They didn't always stick by those guidelines—especially the second one—but just knowing specifics helped them define whether a particular action or retort was falling outside the parameters of our family rules. I also wanted them to *think* in the midst of their arguments and then choose to respond calmly rather than just wildly lashing out. It's amazing that those two simple rules helped them do exactly that.

An Encouraging Hug

Honey, even well-brought-up siblings will
occasionally argue.

63

Odd and Even

And pray that we may be delivered from wicked and evil men, for not everyone has faith.

2 Thessalonians 3:2

Jay and Holly were always arguing over whose turn it was to sit in the front seat. In fact they'd sprint the last few yards to the car door and, according to their self-imposed rule, yell, "Mine!"

But this merely caused more arguments, so I came up with the idea of "odd and even." Jay was born on October 5, so on the odd-numbered days of the month, he sat up front. Holly was born on February 18, so on the even-numbered days of the month, it was her turn to sit up front. We also used that schedule to determine who would be the main dinner and clean-up helper. Of course Jay quickly figured out that the months with thirty-one days gave him an extra day of work. But I just as quickly pointed out it also gave him the opportunity to sit in the front seat two days in a row.

Somehow we got through those days, and they grew into fine young adults. But they remembered. In fact, when they were both home for a college break, we decided to go out to dinner together in my car. As we entered the garage, both suddenly lunged toward the front car door, calling, "Mine!" Jay won, but they took a moment to grin at each other as friends, remembering those long-ago days when they had raced for the front seat in earnest competition.

Perhaps the "odd and even" system won't work in your family. So come up with an idea that *will* work, perhaps by asking your children for their ideas. Believe me, there is a solution to sibling arguments.

An Encouraging Hug

Honey, sometimes you have to get a little creative in solving arguments.

64

Praying for Strangers

Do not let any unwholesome talk come out of your mouths,
but only what is helpful for building others up according
to their needs, that it may benefit those who listen.

Ephesians 4:29

Ruth said when she was growing up, her mother—as they drove on errands—would often point out individuals on the sidewalk, reminding young Ruth to pray for them.

Once Ruth commented on a man who was staggering out of a bar. Ruth's mother had been concentrating on a truck on her left and had not yet noticed the man. But at Ruth's comment about the man's drunkenness, her mother gently said, "Don't ridicule him; pray for him—and pray for his family too."

Ruth is now a middle-aged grandmother but says that lesson has never left her. She told me the story years ago, but I remembered it and tried to teach my children to pray for strangers as well. And I still have opportunities to put the idea into practice.

In fact just recently, while adjusting my window blinds for the day, I heard a screech of tires and then loud cursing. From my second-story position, I could look across my tiny backyard into the parking lot of adjacent town houses. There I saw the driver of a grocery truck standing outside his vehicle yelling into his cell phone. In his slamming on the brakes, one of the bread shelves had emptied itself into the passenger area of his truck and several loaves had fallen onto the pavement. As he continued to yell into the phone, he picked up each loaf of bread and spiked it into the back of the truck. I had two simultaneous thoughts: (1) *I'm glad he's not my delivery man,* and (2) *I wonder what's happened.* Then I finally began to pray for him, asking for the Lord's calm and peace in this situation I had no clue about.

After the man had picked up all of the bread—and bounced more loaves off the inside of the truck—he kicked the right front tire several times, yelled a goodbye into the phone, and got back into his vehicle, burning rubber all the way down the drive. Undoubtedly I'll never know why he was so irritated, but that's the wonderful thing about prayer. We don't have to know the details.

Many of my friends and I use the sound of sirens as a reminder to be praying not only for the injured people and their rescuers but also for young men and women involved in public protection. I pray for a young policewoman in Michigan and a fire captain in California.

Again, we don't need to know the details of the situation; we just need to trust the One who does know.

An Encouraging Hug

Honey, help your children develop the lifelong habit of praying for strangers.

65

Special Time

Be completely humble and gentle; be patient, bearing with one another in love.

Ephesians 4:2

Believe it or not, children have stresses in their young lives. And it isn't going to help them one bit if you constantly point out all of *your* stresses. Saying you have greater stress doesn't lessen theirs. That's like claiming that because you have a smashed leg, their smashed finger shouldn't hurt. Nope, life doesn't work that way. Pain is pain. And often children will act out their pain by arguing with each other.

So start defusing the situation by getting them to talk. Or if they're young, have them draw or use other visual techniques. I know of one teacher who taught her students to spread their arms to correspond to what they were feeling. Thus a child might say, "I'm feeling this much angry," and spread her arms very wide. Or "I'm only this much happy," and hold her hands closer together. The teacher has found that as children have an opportunity and an avenue to express their feelings appropriately, they are far less likely to express those feelings *in*appropriately.

I've also learned that kids will fight more when they aren't getting enough time with their parents. When my teens were busy with school activities during the week, we used Sunday afternoons for family meeting time. We'd discuss any problems that had come since our last discussion.

In addition, I turned Friday nights totally over to them, alternating Fridays between the two. Giving both children separate time with me let them know they are important as individuals. On the first and third Fridays of the month (again using the "odd and even" system), Jay and I would enjoy an activity of his choice and then end the evening with hamburgers at his favorite restaurant. During one of those evenings, he asked questions about the Vietnam War, which resulted in our taking a four-hour family trip south to see the Vietnam Veterans Memorial in Washington, D.C.

On the second and fourth Fridays, Holly and I would go to her favorite tea shop for dinner—and more conversation. The occasional fifth Friday became family movie night, complete with a rented video and buttered popcorn.

Know what I discovered? Knowing they would have my complete concentration for two full evenings each month cut their arguments way down. They no longer had to fight for my attention. Now, if your children are younger, you may have to set aside one evening each week for each child. You don't have to leave the house or make a big deal out of it. Just something as simple as allowing the child to stay up an extra thirty or sixty minutes with you once a week may be all that is needed. But for this to work, you have to make sure you keep your agreement to set aside that evening for the child. If those promised evenings get lost in the shuffle of unexpected activities, then you will merely create greater problems for yourself.

An Encouraging Hug

Honey, spending special time with each child will be special for you as well.

66

Practicing for the Future

Be devoted to one another in brotherly love. Honor one another above yourselves.

Romans 12:10

The "easy road" of out-shouting the kids, slapping them into silence, or being sarcastic is not the best road. Control is achieved not by holding your child under your thumb but by responding in such a calm and loving way that your child can't fight you.

As my children got older, I stressed they should see their response to each other as practice for marriage. So, for example, when they were working on a household project together and Holly was irritated because Jay didn't anticipate what she needed him to do, I reminded her to state her expectations specifically—and that her future husband wouldn't read her mind either.

And when Jay wondered why she got upset when he left the newspaper all over the kitchen counter, I reminded him that folding it back up is not only courteous but good practice for when he's married.

Occasionally I had an opportunity to see my advice bear good fruit. Early one summer day, Jay's friend Mike was helping us move Holly back home from college. She'd shared an apartment with two other young women and had to rearrange her old room at home to fit in the second twin bed she'd used at school. Jay and Mike dutifully placed the second bed just where she had asked. But as she studied the room configuration for a moment, she decided she wanted both beds along the walls and asked the guys to please move them.

Jay bent forward to grab the headboard, but Mike threw his arms up. "Wait a minute, Holly," he said. "We just moved it the way you wanted it in the first place."

Holly nodded. "I know. But I don't like it that way."

Mike wouldn't budge. "Why didn't you have us move it where you wanted it to begin with?"

She looked bewildered. "I didn't know I wasn't going to like it that way."

Jay interrupted with a chuckle. "Aw, come on, Mike. Think of this as practice for when you're married. Grab the bottom of the bed."

Mike complied but added one more grumble: "If this is a taste of marriage, I'm never getting married."

Jay and Holly just looked at each other and grinned.

An Encouraging Hug

Honey, remember what they say:
"Practice makes perfect."

67

Volunteer Workers

If anyone has material possessions and sees his brother in need but has no pity on him, how can the love of God be in him?

1 John 3:17

Cassie and Dan hated to admit it, but their three children were starting to turn into self-centered, materialistic brats. They tried scolding them, talking to them, selecting Scripture for family devotions illustrating the importance of having a servant's heart, but nothing made a dent in their attitude. Then Cassie heard that the local soup kitchen needed volunteer workers for the evening meals. With Dan's encouragement, she signed the five of them up for three months of cooking and serving on Thursday nights. Cassie likes helping others, but she confesses her motivation wasn't pure; she wanted their children to see how easy they had it.

Of course the kids grumbled at first, but gradually, as they got to know the regulars and saw the encouragement the evening program gave the street people, they began to look forward to Thursdays. The hoped-for change in their attitude came as they saw families eat at the soup kitchen before going to the nearby shelter to spend the night.

"Where do the kids do homework?" their middle son asked.

"Don't they have toys?" their youngest son asked.

But the greatest change occurred in their oldest child, a daughter, who stopped demanding expensive name-brand jeans and began to use her baby-sitting money to buy books to read to the children each Thursday.

An Encouraging Hug

Honey, find ways for your family to volunteer together to help others.

68

Look around You

In everything set them an example by doing what is good. In your teaching show integrity, seriousness and sound- ness of speech.

Titus 2:7–8

Obviously not every family experiences dramatic changes in their children's attitudes just because they start help- ing others. But often that's an important start.

Tina and Shawn introduced their children early to the concept of thinking of others by having them take computer-generated large-print Scripture verses to the folks at a nearby convalescent home. One week their six-year-old daughter took her box of crayons too and asked the recipients to color the letters with her. They were delighted and told her about their own childhood as they bent over the page.

"Halloween caroling" was a big thing for the Stamps family during the five years they lived in a rough Los Angeles neighborhood. Several days ahead of time, Mary would hand out letters in the neighborhood that said, "Halloween means a lot of things to a lot of people. To some it's a night to dress up and ask for candy. To some it's a night of dark deeds that can't even be spoken of. To some it's a night of mischief and pranks. But for us, Halloween means 'Holy Eve' and is a reminder that the Lord is going to return soon. Until he comes back, we hope he can look at our neighborhood and find people loving him and loving one another." Then she'd explain that the family would be out that evening serenading their neighbors with worship songs.

On "Holy Eve," the daughters dressed up as the bride of Christ. (At that time, there weren't any sons.) Then, accompanied by their guitar-strumming dad and singing mother, the little "brides" handed out candy wrapped in Scripture verses.

Mary says, "In those five years, we made a difference in our rough neighborhood by showing the love of Christ."

What's the goal of *your* family—to collect the most toys or to help others? If you want to help others, have you found a ministry that fits your busy schedule and your family's personality?

Several doctors here in Colorado Springs take their families to Third World countries once a year for three weeks of temporary medical duty. Other families open their homes to foreign students studying at local universities. Even the simple act of inviting a student into your home for a meal can have a long-lasting impact. In fact I often think of Fuchida, who returned to Japan in the 1930s, embittered because not one American family had invited him into their home during his four lonely years here. When his nation later asked him to lead the attack on Pearl Harbor, he accepted without hesitation.

I also remember Mangusto, the young African who encountered only prejudice here. When he came into power in his own country, he expelled missionaries and welcomed the Marxists, who eventually toppled the traditional government of Ethiopia, the world's oldest Christian nation.

Oh, the difference one family serving the Lord might have made!

An Encouraging Hug

Honey, you can make a big difference in this world, starting in your own neighborhood.

69

A Spare Bed

*Call upon me in the day of trouble; I will deliver you, and
you will honor me.*

Psalm 50:15

A Michigan father, John, says he hates to think where
he'd be today if his best friend's parents hadn't taken him
in during his last two years of high school. His mother
had died several years before, and his father's drinking
had escalated to the point where he had actually threatened John's life.

When John moved in, his new "parents" set forth the
ground rules. He would abide by the same rules they set
for their son, including faithful church attendance. He
agreed, came to the Lord within a few months, and is
today a spiritually solid husband and father.

My venture into taking one of Holly's friends into our
home wasn't quite as dramatic or successful, but I'm
still glad we tried.

During Holly's sophomore year, her friend, whom I'll call Heidi, began to confide in me about her home life. Her mother, who had been married and divorced three times, often left Heidi alone for several days at a time and occasionally became physically aggressive when arguing with her.

When Heidi asked me if she could come live with us, I knew we would be moving in the near future and wasn't comfortable making a permanent arrangement. But I was certainly open to a short-term stay that would give her and her mother some breathing space. Jay, Holly, and I prayed about it before I called Heidi's mother and offered to provide a buffer zone while they considered family counseling.

Her mother readily agreed, saying Heidi was never satisfied. Heidi, in turn, said her mother never spent time with her. And both insisted everything would be all right if the other one would just shape up. As I talked with Heidi, I made it clear I would expect her to adhere to the same household rules (including faithful church attendance) Jay and Holly followed. She agreed.

My prayer that night was, "Lord, we really need your help here. I don't want to be caught in my old patterns, always trying to rescue others, but I also don't want to withhold shelter and your encouragement from Heidi. Lord, please give me your direction. I can't solve her problems, and I have no power to straighten out her situation—only you can do that. I'm thankful Heidi sees our home as one filled with peace and love, but don't let me get so caught in the flattery that I miss your voice."

I picked up Heidi the following Friday. During her time with us, she followed my rules, pitched in around the house, and joined us for devotions and three weekly church services in addition to attending counseling with her mother. But I also found that as she became more comfortable with us, she began to encourage Holly to challenge my authority. "She can't tell you to do that," she'd say, or, as the cross-country move loomed, "She's ruining your life."

It took constant discussions and much prayer to hold a steady course during her stay with us. It was hard to have another person in the house, especially one with so many needs, but the experience stretched our James 1:22–24 muscles: "Do not merely listen to the word, and so deceive yourselves. Do what it says. Anyone who listens to the word but does not do what it says is like a man who looks at his face in a mirror and, after looking at himself, goes away and immediately forgets what he looks like."

By obeying God's Word, we came away with a new appreciation for each other. Would I do it again? In a heartbeat.

An Encouraging Hug

Honey, sometimes obeying God's Word means we have to stretch our spiritual muscles.

70

A Hand to Wave

See that you do not look down on one of these little ones.
For I tell you that their angels in heaven always see the
face of my Father in heaven.

Matthew 18:10

Recently an elementary school principal asked a local
pastor if some members of the congregation would be
willing to walk by the playground at recess and wave
at designated children who needed to know somebody
cared about them!

Such stories are not new to Dr. Virgil Gulker, executive
director of Kids Hope USA, based in Holland, Michigan.
He helps folks reach out to at-risk children. His meth-
ods are simple—match a hurting child with a church
volunteer—adult or youth—who will encourage that
youngster, tutor him, and treat him kindly.

He constantly stresses that the church must form relationships with hurting children. "We don't need more
programs," he says. "We need *people* who care enough

to put an arm around a child before we lose him or her to drugs, gangs, or despair. If the church doesn't get involved in the lives of hurting children, we will lose an entire generation."

A superintendent of schools liked Virgil's idea so much he decided to read a story to the kindergarten class once a week. After his first time there, a little girl took his face in her hands and said with wonder, "Is this what it's like to have a daddy?"

After a school in Allegan, Michigan, implemented Virgil's method, the principal wrote to Virgil saying, "I am seeing these students less frequently in the office for discipline problems. For example, two of the boys who are part of the program used to be sent almost daily to the office for some type of trouble they were getting into. But since they started meeting with their tutors, they haven't been sent to the office once for misbehavior."

Yes, Christ's people can make a difference. And notice that none of the school administrators are crying "separation of church and state" here.

An Encouraging Hug

Honey, sometimes the smallest gestures can make the greatest difference.

71

Easing a Child's Stress

*Therefore, as God's chosen people, holy and dearly loved,
clothe yourselves with compassion, kindness, humility,
gentleness and patience.*

Colossians 3:12

Sometimes people fantasize about the "good old days"
when life was simpler. But stress has always been a major
part of human life—all the way back to the days when we
had to live off the land while dealing with wild animals,
human enemies, disease, and natural disasters.

After my grandparents married in 1909, their first
home was a simple cabin. One morning Mama picked
up the pillow to make the bed and discovered a black
snake! Her shriek brought Papa running in from the
woodpile, ax in hand.

We may not have snakes under our pillows today,
but stress is still a reality. Here are a few reminders for
helping children deal with it.

Use "letting go" signals. When I catch myself being tense, I turn my palms down and say, "Let it go, San. Let it go."

Once I've "emptied" my hands, then I can turn them back up, asking the Lord to fill them with what he wants. I also tell myself, "You *can* do this. Deep breath." And sure enough, I can. Even toddlers can be taught to take that deep breath before giving in to their temper.

Insist on rest. We're prone to mistakes if we're suffering from a lack of sleep. That's why the government regulates the amount of time pilots can work each month, because if pilots are fatigued, it may result in loss of human life. Now, most of us don't have jobs that involve life-and-death crises, but if we're tired, we're not going to respond the way we should to the folks around us. And neither will our children.

Provide proper nourishment. When I taught high school, more than a few of my students came to morning classes having eaten only a sugary donut. Some had cola with their donut. I'd just shake my head, because I knew the teens had made that choice themselves.

But the situations that make me the saddest are when young children are given the wrong fuels in the morning. Recently early one morning a mother and her two young children were in front of me in a checkout line. They all had cinnamon rolls and little bottles of sweetened juice—sugars that were sending them into the day.

Now, I know how difficult it is to get everyone out the door to school and to work on time, but I also know that our bodies can't run on empty. I'm not advocating the big breakfasts of eggs, sausage, biscuits, and gravy my grandmother and mother prepared during our long-ago farming days, but even a slice of whole wheat toast spread with peanut butter can provide fuel to keep a child alert. In addition to a solid, nonsugar cereal, keep fruit, flavored yogurt, or boiled eggs on hand. I know of one creative mother who lets her children dye eggs Easter-style every couple of weeks so they will be excited about eating them. Just as we teach our children the importance of brushing their teeth and dressing appropriately each morning, we can teach them the importance of grabbing a quick but nutritious breakfast, which will go a long way toward lessening stress.

An Encouraging Hug

Honey, stress has always been with us, but it does not have to run our lives.

72

The Three Cs

His compassions never fail. They are new every morning;
great is your faithfulness.

Lamentations 3:22–23

Several years ago I had the privilege of working on
an article with Jim Broome, cofounder of the Detroit-
based Alcoholics for Christ. From him, I learned that
an alcoholic's family is often controlled by the one who
is the most out of control—the alcoholic.

Jim says, "One of the first things we tell families is,
'You didn't *cause* the alcoholism, you can't *control* it, and
you can't *cure* it.' That's profoundly simple—but also
hard to sell sometimes, because the alcoholic blames
everyone else for his drinking: stress at work, big disappointments, his childhood, even the children's normal
daily noise. Everything becomes a reason, an excuse to
drink."

The unfortunate part is that the alcoholic becomes the
leader of the family because everything revolves around

whether or not he's drinking. Think about that—the *sick* one becomes the leader!

Jim continues, "Children of the alcoholic will follow the strongest person in the family—which is usually the problem drinker. The girls often marry an alcoholic or a dominating man because they don't know what normal family life is. Most of them, after putting up with so much garbage during the important growing years, have such a low opinion of themselves they think they don't deserve any better. The idea of a family being a team and working things out together is foreign to them."

So how does this apply to our parenting? First of all, whether or not we grew up with an alcoholic in our home, we need to be aware that our decisions profoundly affect our children and, in turn, the generations to follow. But the encouraging part is that we don't have to be bound by those old patterns, and we aren't programmed to thrust our own childhood hurts onto our children. Jesus died for those hurts—and offers us freedom from them. No matter what your childhood was like, be encouraged. Your children can be blessed and, in turn, bless others.

An Encouraging Hug

Honey, remember, you didn't cause the addiction, you can't control it, and you can't cure it.

73

Stress Relievers

Forget the former things; do not dwell on the past. See, I am doing a new thing! Now it springs up; do you not perceive it? I am making a way in the desert and streams in the wasteland.

Isaiah 43:18–19

Stress and I are old buddies, but over the years I've learned a few things to help loosen the knots in my emotional shoulders. Perhaps some of them will help you as well.

Start with prayer. True, God knows our situation, but something freeing happens when we hear ourselves verbalizing the problem. His shoulders are pretty big, so we can even complain to him in great detail. I love it that when the Lord said, "Come to me," he *didn't* add, "But make sure you come without tears and with a right attitude."

After you've stated everything he already knows, hang around just to listen for a while to whatever thoughts he drops into your spirit.

Exercise. Even a quick walk is a great way to burn off stress. Often there's a tendency for a child under stress to pull away from friends and after-school activities. Encourage your children to let off pent-up steam by keeping active.

Say no *more often.* Parents as well as kids have to concentrate on this one. If we parents are involved in too many things, we'll be running in forty-seven different directions. And if the house isn't calm, then the kids are going to pick up on it and experience their own stress.

Keep a detailed family calendar. Pity the poor family driver who realizes at the last minute she has to have her children in three different spots at four o'clock that afternoon. If you post each family member's schedule on the calendar at the beginning of the week, things won't be forgotten and you can avoid a major crisis.

Plan ahead. Any time we talk about whittling down stress, we always talk about planning ahead. But it works! So the night before, make sure you have the school bags and lunches packed. And there's no rule saying the parent has to do all this either. I believe in child labor and think kids should pack their own lunches the night before. They should also plan what they're going to wear the next day. That way, they'll know if all the parts of a particular outfit are washed, mended, and readily available, and there's no yelling, "Mom! Where are my green socks?"

Relax your standards. Yes, you can have a less-than-perfect house. Is anyone really going to notice that your door handles need polishing or that your pan bottoms aren't shining? For years I had all my copper cooking pans hanging in the kitchen. It bothered me if they weren't shiny, so I spent a lot of time making sure they were. Finally, I had the good sense to store them in the cabinet—out of my sight as well as my guests'—and spend that extra time with my family.

Hire out the hateful jobs. What chore do you absolutely hate doing? For me, it's scrubbing carpets. I'm a strong woman, so I can certainly lug a heavy carpet-cleaning machine around, but the last time I tried it, I wound up sitting on the stairs, crying in frustration. There's nothing wrong with hiring out the chores that are overwhelming for you. And if you can't afford to hire the help, offer to trade work with a friend.

Count your blessings. If we allow ourselves to concentrate on what we have *lost* instead of what we have *left,* we're headed for trouble. Marlene taught her five-year-old to thank the Lord for three new things every morning before breakfast. They both had so much fun thinking of new—often silly—items that they went into the day smiling.

Unclutter your life. Get rid of junk. Much of the stress of cleaning comes from having to deal with all of our stuff. Giving away items that are merely taking up shelf space (think of it as recycling) or holding a major garage sale to free up more space is worth the effort. And less-cluttered rooms are not only easier to clean but are also calming. Introduce your children to the concept of giving some of their toys to a women and children's shelter—but let them choose which things to give away.

Analyze and adjust. Ask yourself, "What purpose does this activity serve for the family?" If it's just adding more frustration to an already crowded schedule, then ditch it. But if it truly is important for the family, then ask yourself what other activity you can cut to spend more time with this one.

Accept what you can't change. Sometimes we need to remember the serenity prayer: "God grant me the serenity to accept the things I cannot change, the courage to change the things I can, and the wisdom to know the difference."

My Kentucky grandmother, Mama Farley, would often say, "There are some things in life that all you can do with 'em is bear 'em." I agree. But for all the rest, let's do our part to put stress relievers into action.

An Encouraging Hug

Honey, stress is part of our human condition. But you can do your part to keep it from becoming overwhelming.

74

Signs of Stress

He makes me lie down in green pastures, he leads me beside quiet waters, he restores my soul.

Psalm 23:2–3

Sometimes parents are so caught up in their own concerns that they aren't aware of the stress with which their child may be dealing. And just because a child isn't yelling doesn't mean he or she isn't under stress. So to help you be more conscious of your child's internal struggles, I've listed a few stress symptoms. Don't use this list to make a diagnosis, but it may help you be specific when you present your concerns to your family physician.

- Unexplained aching muscles, especially back or neck pain
- Pounding heart
- Frequent headaches or stomachaches (Boy, do I remember that one. When I was in first grade, I

got a stomachache every morning. No wonder. A "big girl" in fifth grade threatened every day to beat me up.)

- Restlessness
- Impulsive, uncontrolled eating
- Difficulty concentrating
- Difficulty sleeping or staying awake
- Chronic irritability or repeated displays of irritating behavior
- Lack of energy
- Nail biting, hair pulling, other tics
- Frequent outbursts of anger
- Withdrawal (If your child is naturally a loner, you may not notice anything unusual about this pattern. Just be sensitive to any out-of-the-norm behavior.)

If you notice any of these patterns, talk to your child— and listen to his or her concerns. Many times as we listen, we learn about specific struggles and are better able to offer help.

An Encouraging Hug

Honey, a few minutes each day of talking with your child makes all the difference in the world.

75

Dump the Guilt

If we confess our sins, he is faithful and just and will forgive us our sins and purify us from all unrighteousness.

1 John 1:9

Working mothers seem to feel more guilt than dads. For some women, it's because they're emotionally bound to the way they've been taught things should be—men are the breadwinners and women are at their children's beck and call. If guilt made us better parents, we'd be all set; but guilt actually makes us worse parents. Often we just add more stress to our life and wind up falsely thinking we can buy things for our children to make up for not being home more often. Don't get caught in that emotional trap.

I hope it's obvious I'm talking about "normal" parenting guilt here, not the deep-rooted stuff that may need the help of a godly professional. If you're struggling in this area, you may want to consider the difference between three types of guilt—true, false, and misplaced.

True guilt results when we've done something wrong and need to confess it, starting with asking the Lord for forgiveness. First John 1:9 says, "If we confess our sins, he is faithful and just and will forgive us our sins and purify us from all unrighteousness."

Then we need to ask forgiveness from the ones we've wronged—often our children. For many adults, that's harder than asking God! But unless we offer habitual or insincere apologies, our children will forgive us.

False guilt comes when we think we can control every detail of our child's life, often overburdening ourselves in an attempt to make life "perfect." You can test yourself for false guilt by listening to how often you use "should" or "ought," as in "Jamie should have a homemade costume for the party," or "I ought to iron Johnny's underwear too."

Misplaced guilt comes when a normally unimportant event turns into a crisis. For example, we can send our child to the corner store for bread forty-seven times and not think a thing about it. But if his leg is broken on the forty-eighth trip, the incident may become, in our mind, *our* fault rather than the fault of the idiot who ran the stop sign.

God uses true guilt to call us back to fellowship with him. Satan uses false and misplaced guilt to preoccupy us with emotional regrets. After all, as long as we're beating ourselves up, he doesn't have to. So let's dump the guilt and enjoy being the parents we were called to be.

An Encouraging Hug

Honey, don't beat yourself up over every little thing. It's okay not to be perfect.

76

No Raving Beauty

*Why are you downcast, O my soul? Why so disturbed
within me? Put your hope in God, for I will yet praise him,
my Savior and my God.*

Psalm 42:5–6

The Proverbs 31 Woman gets hauled out every Mother's
Day in many churches across the country and held up as
the perfect woman—a vast challenge for every mother.
Know what I love? She's never described as having physical beauty. It is her concern for others and her good
work habits that have given her this prominent place
in Scripture.

As I speak at conferences and retreats, I'm aware of
how much the media has defined even the believer's
concept of what a Christian woman should look like.
And too often, instead of emphasizing pure thoughts
and healthy habits, even churches present the idea that
our "temple" is to be translated into bodily perfection.
Kind of like a Barbie with a Bible!

It is that very concept that almost kept me from having a public ministry. How could I, a feisty mountain woman with wide hips, stand before audiences and tell them about the glories of the Lord? And did the Lord really want me to do that? After all, I had been born weighing a whopping eleven pounds, eight ounces. If he wanted me in the public eye, wouldn't he have made sure I was born at a more normal weight? Of course I hadn't learned yet that he isn't bound by a particular culture's concept of beauty. So I continued to struggle, content to hide in my pew and allow the enemy to keep whispering his lies that only perfect folks dare to have a public ministry.

Of course, when we believe we have no worth, there will always be folks around us who, perhaps because of their own feelings of worthlessness, are only too happy to confirm our image of ourselves. Perhaps it was about the time my husband, Don, was diagnosed with brain cancer and I had to take over so many of the decisions—medically as well as in the home—that I started seeing my worth. Gradually I learned I was capable of making good decisions and capable of getting things accomplished.

Then, when Don died, every decision was suddenly in my lap. I couldn't hide out, but even as various friends began to invite me to give my testimony at their churches, I hesitated. But my prayer had been that the Lord would bring his good out of my pain, so I had to go. Gradually more invitations came from churches a little farther out of my area. Soon I had a speaking ministry. Still, it took me a long while to accept the opportunities the Lord was offering.

Gradually, though, I stopped worrying about what I looked like and started thinking about the challenges the people in my audience face. Then, after a wonderful time at a California event in which the audience laughed and cried at my many stories, the elegant and, of course, slim wife of one of the local pastors approached me.

"You know, dear," she began. "You really are heavy. You should think about losing weight. You have kind of a pretty face and would look really nice if you were slim."

I turned to her, amazed she felt "led" to inform me of my size. Did she think I don't look in the mirror? It crossed my feisty little mind to clutch at my chest, reel backward, and shriek, "What?! I'm fat?! Oh, thank you for telling me!" But I thought my less-than-saintly sarcasm undoubtedly would go right over her head. Still, I was irritated by the thought that my value goes up as my hip size goes down. In other words, her "helpful" comments pushed my emotional feisty button to the limit. So as sweetly as I could, I smiled and said, "*Kind of* a pretty face? Honey, if I lost weight, I'd be breaking up marriages. In fact I'm probably saving *yours* right now!"

Her eyes widened as she clamped her mouth shut. I'm sure that was the last time she felt compelled to inform a woman about her size!

So, mothers—and dads—rejoice in who God has created you to be. And pass on that same self-confidence to your children.

An Encouraging Hug

Honey, you have great value—no matter your size.

77

First Aid and CPR

Therefore keep watch, because you do not know the day or the hour.

Matthew 25:13

Recently I took a Red Cross first aid and CPR course with the hope I'll never need to use it. But as my family expands and potential health problems arise, I want to be sure that if there is a crisis, I won't be the one standing uselessly by and wringing her hands.

I confess I watched the first aid videos with their realistic dramatizations of home and workplace crises through my fingers. But I had enough situations when my children were growing up that I know awful things do happen. Once, I even had to drive my daughter, with a deeply cut leg, to the hospital twenty minutes away, but I wasn't tempted to faint *until* I knew the child was safely in the hands of the emergency room doctor.

But I'm older now and I know I need more than just sheer grit to help me meet any potential problem. First aid is exactly that—the *first* help given to a person. But unless we are calm and correctly trained to respond in an appropriate way, we can cause more harm than good. I still remember as a child seeing a mother running up the church sidewalk holding her little boy who had just been hit by a car. He should not have been moved, but in her panic, she swooped him up and ran for help instead of allowing help to come to him.

I also remember a coworker, who, I am convinced, would have survived his basketball heart attack if his playing partners had known CPR. Instead, there was just a great deal of panic and waiting for the ambulance to arrive. Of course there are no guarantees just because we know CPR and have taken a first aid course. But chances of a recovery are better if someone is present who can help the injured person.

Even very young children can be taught simple rules, such as Stop, Drop, and Roll if your clothing catches on fire. And children love practicing. An older child can be taught where the pressure point is in the upper arm and leg to push the artery against the bone to stop severe bleeding. During my long-ago high school first aid course, we were taught to make a tourniquet using a belt or our thigh-high nylons. (Of course the young men in the class liked that.) However, the use of a tourniquet is no longer taught in first aid courses.

Check with your local Red Cross or YMCA for their offerings in family first aid, even as you hope you'll never have to use the skills you learn. I'd rather have the knowledge and never use it than wish, in a time of crisis, that I knew what to do.

An Encouraging Hug

Honey, invest a few hours in preparation
for potential problems.

78

Appropriate Energy

Be very careful, then, how you live—not as unwise but as wise.

Ephesians 5:15

An important lifelong lesson we can pass along to our children is to help them learn to deal with the consequences of their actions. For Peggy, that started when her son, Charles, was two. She gave him a frozen treat, which he licked and then waved about before taking the next bite.

"Don't wave it like that, honey," she said. "It will fall off the stick."

But of course he didn't listen, and sure enough, the frozen orange treat fell onto the grass. He asked for another.

"No, honey, I'm sorry," she replied. "But that's what happens when you aren't careful."

You're probably thinking, *Oh, come on. That's a little extreme.* Okay, perhaps. But where *do* we as parents start to teach our kids that not everything in this world is replaceable? When he's six and has just broken an expensive toy? When she's nine and has gotten grass stains on her dress because she refused to change her clothes after church? When he's eleven and has just broken your great-grandmother's fruit bowl while batting a ball around the house? When she's sixteen and has just wrecked the family car even though you warned her repeatedly about speeding on icy streets? I prefer teaching that lesson earlier, while the consequences—and the resulting stress—are less severe.

Recently thirteen-year-old Andy was suspended from riding the school bus for a week because of misconduct. His mother, Allison, had to leave for work each morning at 5:45, so she wasn't available to drive him. It crossed her mind to ask the neighbors to take him, but then she decided now was a good time to introduce him to the "consequences of action" philosophy. She informed him he'd have to walk to school.

"What? You're kidding," he said. "That's three miles. I can't be late to class!"

Allison nodded. "Well, then you'll have to get up earlier and start walking by seven o'clock."

Andy did exactly that—and was never again suspended from the bus for misconduct.

When I taught in Michigan, we occasionally had parents in the office, demanding the bus driver's job and threatening to sue because the student was being denied his rights to an education, yelling that it was the school's responsibility to make sure he got there, and so on. They refused to see it was the student's responsibility to obey the rules.

Jim, a principal I worked with for a while, said that in his thirty years in the high school—first as a teacher and later as an administrator—he had seen the same rebellious types ("punks" he called them) in the hallways, just with a different hairstyle over the years. He said the only difference in the situation was the parent's attitude. Most of the parents in the 1950s would tell the school to "nail" their kid, and then he'd be in even greater trouble once he got home. But years later parents were accompanied by their lawyers when they came to meetings with the principal.

I remember more than one abusive educator from my own school days, so I'm not saying all teachers should have unlimited power over a student. But I am saying that one of the many problems in our society is the lack of respect for authority and parents who too quickly say, "Not *my* child."

What goals have you set for your child? I hope the following are included:

- Make your children's souls your first priority—eternity is a reality.
- Choose your battles carefully.
- Know your children's struggles.
- Train them for adulthood—including teaching respect for authority.
- Establish early that you are the parent and the one who must stand before God to give an account for your parenting.
- Remind them that today's choices set tomorrow's direction.

An Encouraging Hug

Honey, put your energy into the things that truly matter.
Don't "die" on every emotional hill.

79

Watching Out for Each Other

A new command I give you: Love one another. As I have
loved you, so you must love one another. By this all men
will know that you are my disciples, if you love one
another.

John 13:34–35

A while back I visited my parents in Michigan the same
week a cousin and his wife and children were there. The
oldest son, Levi, age ten, has assumed the role his name
suggests—that of spiritual leader for his seven younger
brothers and sister.

One evening, Hannah, five years old and the only girl,
watched me put on lipstick before I left for dinner. As
I saw her lean against the full-length mirror to look up
at me, I remembered a scene from my own childhood—
watching one of my older cousins, Joyce, get dressed for
a date. To my delight, Joyce had leaned over and gently
applied a dab of pink lipstick on my six-year-old lips.

Still remembering that sensation of being all grown-
up, I leaned toward Hannah and whispered, "Would you
like to have some lipstick?"

Her eyes widened with pleasure, just as I'm sure mine did those years ago when Joyce had asked me the same question. As I bent down, lipstick tube extended, Levi was at my elbow.

"Our mother doesn't want her to wear lipstick," he said in his best ten-year-old authoritarian voice.

I wasn't about to mess with someone else's parental decisions, so as Hannah glared at her brother, I turned to him.

"Levi, I appreciate your stopping me from doing something your mother doesn't approve of. I would have made a mistake. Thank you."

He nodded his head in a forgiving but don't-let-it-happen-again way and went back to the board game he and the others had been playing. Hannah continued to fume at her brother while I stroked her hair. I hope I'm privileged to see what these delightful children will be like in ten years.

A while back Jay and Holly were in downtown Colorado Springs after a concert. Back then they were still in that stage where they didn't walk together, so he was several paces behind her. Then as she started to pass in front of a guy leaning against the building, Jay was immediately beside her—and between her and the man.

She told me about it later. Since I believe good deeds should be acknowledged as an encouragement to our children to continue making the right choices, I told Jay that Holly and I both appreciated his looking out for her. Jay, in typical male fashion, brushed it off with a shrug. "Well, the guy did give me pause," was all he said.

Two different situations, but two brothers showed their concern for their sisters.

An Encouraging Hug

Honey, be encouraged. Our children often come through for each other at the most unexpected times.

80

Constant Prayer

Pray continually.

1 Thessalonians 5:17

I'm grateful to be on this side of single parenting now that Jay and Holly are grown. I will have to give an account to God for my decisions that influenced them up to adulthood, but now they'll have to give their own account. Whew!

But I still wrap constant prayers around them. One March afternoon a while back, I was in my office after Holly left to go back to college. I glanced at the clock at one point, expecting her to call soon to let me know she had arrived safely. Suddenly I was compelled to pray for her protection—asking that angels surround her car.

A few minutes later, to my great relief, the phone rang. But as soon as I heard her voice, I knew something was wrong. She proceeded to tell me that just ten minutes earlier she had been sitting at a stoplight near her school, waiting to turn left. As she watched, a driver sped through the caution light just as another car across the intersection was turning. With a deafening impact, the speeding car clipped the fender of the turning car—and tossed it airborne.

There was no place for Holly to turn her car. All she could do was watch the airborne car come right at her. In horror, she clapped her hands over her mouth, expecting the car to crash into hers. Instead, the vehicle dropped just a foot in front of her hood!

Immediately other drivers were out of their cars, cell phones in hand, calling the police and administering first aid. One big guy directed traffic and waved Holly through. She drove the short distance to school and promptly called me.

When I told her a sudden impulse to pray for her had come over me at the time of the accident, we both cried.

I didn't hear about an incident Jay had until several weeks after it happened.

He began his report with "The business is over and nobody was hurt, so don't get upset."

Well, as soon as I heard "don't get upset," I started getting upset. He told me he had been waiting at a light downtown when a guy in a sporty car pulled up next to him and sneered at Jay's ancient car.

Jay was in one of those macho moods, so he sneered back. The guy pulled a gun from under his front seat, pointed it, and asked, "You got a problem?"

Jay immediately said, "Heck, no!" The light changed then, and they both drove off.

That explains the times I suddenly start praying for him.

I pray for my family constantly, but I don't understand why sometimes I'm called to prayer and the accident still occurs. All I know is that I'm supposed to pray—and continue to trust the Lord to provide his calm harbor for us all.

An Encouraging Hug

Honey, want to worry less? Then pray more.

81

Anxious for Nothing

Do not be anxious about anything, but in everything, by prayer and petition, with thanksgiving, present your requests to God.

Philippians 4:6

Sherry straightened up from wiping her baby's nose yet again and turned to her mother, visiting from the East Coast.

"Did you ever feel as though you'd never survive teething?" she asked.

Her mother nodded. "But when I complained to *my* mother, she just smiled and said, 'All too soon that baby will be a mother herself, asking you the same question.' Sure enough, here we are. I'm glad I listened to her and started enjoying you more instead of thinking about all the work."

Even though Sherry knew she'd just received a gentle lecture, she turned to look at her daughter with new awareness.

Every time we parents turn around, it seems, the latest magazine article hits us with all of the things we have done wrong. If you're feeling a little bombarded lately, let me encourage you to quietly list all the things you've done *right*—starting with the ways you've sheltered, protected, and loved your child. Oh, you may never hear the appreciation you long for (did *you* appreciate all *your* parents did at the time?), but as you concentrate on your strengths rather than your weaknesses, you will know the difference you have made in your child's life.

An Encouraging Hug

Honey, occasionally we get it right, so be gentle with yourself as well as with your child.

82

Choosing What's Important

Let us not become weary in doing good, for at the proper
time we will reap a harvest if we do not give up.

Galatians 6:9

Not long ago a young mother called for my advice about
her desire to get a master's degree that would prepare
her for a career in family service. I could hear her children in the background, so I asked their ages: three, six,
and nine. Instead of rattling off a list of good schools, I
encouraged her in her present job—raising those little
ones to be healthy individuals who will love the Lord,
honor their parents, and be good citizens.

To illustrate my point, I told her that in the 1970s I
had been preparing to start a Ph.D. program (in mythol-
ogy and folklore, of all things!) when I discovered I was
pregnant with our first child. I set that third degree
aside, saying I'd rather have a baby to hug than a piece
of framed paper to hang on the wall. Education *is* important, and I do believe when you educate the woman, you

educate the family. But an advanced degree is not more important than an unborn child. Now I look at Jay and Holly, and I smile at my good decision to concentrate on my family those many years ago.

Then to the young mother I said, "Honey, children are not little weeds that grow by themselves. They need you. There *is* life after age thirty, and you'll have plenty of time to save the world after your children are grown."

Then I rattled off story after story of blessings I would have missed had I not been there for Jay and Holly.

When I paused for breath, I realized she was crying. "You're an answer to prayer," she finally managed to say. "Why isn't anyone telling us these things?"

Well, obviously we are—veteran mothers, pastors, social workers, and various experts, including the famed Dr. Dobson. But for some reason, she didn't hear that message until I confessed my own struggles and right choices.

An Encouraging Hug

Honey, there's no more important job than being a good parent to your children.

83

Tough Decisions

*From the ends of the earth I call to you, I call as my heart
grows faint; lead me to the rock that is higher than I.*

Psalm 61:2

On the day the movers loaded our van for Colorado
Springs, if I could have undone my decision, I would
have. Jay was excited to make the move, but Holly and
several of her friends were in tears. We hugged everyone
good-bye. Then, before we pulled out of the driveway, I
asked that we all stand in a circle for a parting prayer.
Holly rolled her eyes at my suggestion, but one of her
friends steered her to the group. Just as I opened my
mouth to pray, somebody gave a great sob that caused
me to absolutely lose it. Tears rolled down my cheeks
the entire time I prayed.

For the next three days, Holly slept as I drove—refus-
ing to talk to me or to eat. If I asked her a question, she'd
answer through Jay: "Jay, tell Mom I don't care where
she decides to stop for lunch because I'm not hungry."

I tried being understanding, calm, encouraging, and even loving. But by the time we approached Hays, Kansas, I had *had it*. I pulled into a rest stop just outside of town.

As I set the brake, I said, "Jay, why don't you take a walk? Holly and I are going to have a talk."

And so for the next forty minutes, we sat at a picnic table in what must have been ninety-five-degree heat as I reminded her, point by point, of the many ways over the previous months the Lord seemed to be directing us to Colorado. Then I said I know how difficult life's changes are, but we had prayed about this move and had been convinced the Lord was leading. I stressed that her attitude would determine how successful this move would be for her.

"Don't mess it up for yourself before you even get there," I said.

She never commented, so I just said a quick prayer and called Jay back to the car.

Within a few minutes of getting back onto the highway, we stopped at a fruit stand for grapes. As I put away the change, I noticed Holly had taken the produce back to the car and was washing it with the jug of water we always carried. As I watched her do something other than curl up in the backseat, I knew she was going to be fine.

In the weeks ahead, as we gradually settled into our new community, her sense of loss over New York eased. Now she's convinced this was the best possible move we could have made. Whew!

Perhaps you've had a situation like that too. I hope you were loving and understanding, but I hope you also remembered that you are the parent—and the one who must ultimately stand before God and give an account of your decisions. Often our children are frightened of change and can't imagine that life beyond their own circle could ever yield anything good. I'm not suggesting we make all of our decisions with an I'm-the-parent-that's-why attitude. Rather, we must pray fervently, listen to the Lord's instructions, and trust him for our family's future. Sometimes he will ask us to remain patiently in a certain area or job for another year or two. Sometimes he will ask us to move.

If a move is looming in your future, I suggest you not spring the news on your children. One of my childhood friends went home from school for lunch one day and found movers there loading the van. Her parents had hoped to spare her the agony of saying good-bye, but obviously they caused her even deeper pain.

Involve your children in the decision as much as is reasonable for their age. If they're in the last couple of years of high school, you may even want to consider what they want. One of our friends was prepared to turn down a promotion because it would have meant a move to California just before his daughter's senior year.

He mentioned it over dinner, expecting her to sob, "Oh, thank you, Daddy! Thank you!"

Instead, she said, "I hope you accepted!"

Startled, he asked for an explanation. She had recently decided she wanted to attend a California college but would be held back by the out-of-state tuition. By meeting the residency requirement, she would save at least fifty thousand dollars over four years. They moved the next month.

If your children are younger, you may have to create a sense of excitement by having the chamber of commerce in the new town send information to the child. On mortgage-closing day, one wise mother took pictures of the new house, especially her son's new room, along with pictures of the local pool, softball diamond, and the school he would attend. Another mother called the school's principal and asked for possible pen pals so her daughter would go into the area with some ready-made friends.

Gradually all those children made good adjustments.

An Encouraging Hug

Honey, yes, consider the wishes of your child, but remember that you are the parent.

84

Alarm Clock Curfews

Therefore, prepare your minds for action; be self-controlled; set your hope fully on the grace to be given you when Jesus Christ is revealed.

1 Peter 1:13

Believe it or not, children—even teens—appreciate reasonable rules. Setting rules for them and *with* them not only sets boundaries for expected behavior but also shows your kids you care about what they do. More than once when I taught high school, I heard students answer questions about their curfews not with "I don't have one" but with "My parents don't care what time I get in."

When it comes to making rules, the important word is *reasonable.* Of course we parents are frightened by all that's waiting out there for our children, but keeping them locked up in the house will only create resentment. How much better our rules work when the teen is involved in making them, even if the parent merely asks, "What do you think would be a good limit here?" Or my favorite: "What would you do in this situation if you were the parent and I were the child?"

Now, I realize I'm making an assumption that your children are at least reluctantly subject to your authority, not openly rebellious. If they insist on breaking every curfew, disobeying all your rules, and just barely skirting the law (or not), then you need more help than my feeble words can offer. But I'm convinced most teens will follow rules they have helped set, and they will accept the agreed-on consequences, such as grounding or loss of privileges. Jay responded best to loss of computer privileges, while Holly dreaded phone restrictions. And it's important you not wimp out on the punishment! Because my kids knew I'd follow through, I was spared some of the problems other parents experienced after making empty threats.

We meandered along rather nicely until we moved to Colorado. Here, my teens' high school offered numerous evening activities, so their curfew needed to be extended. I usually feel as though I'm going to turn into a pumpkin right around 9:30, so they were staying up later than I could. We discussed various solutions and settled on the bright idea of setting the alarm clock to go off at their curfew time and placing it in the hallway. If they got in before their curfew, they'd turn off the alarm and go to bed. (Of course I'd hear them and call a cheerful—and relieved—good night.) But if the alarm went off, it would awaken me, and I'd be sitting up waiting for the absent child. In all the years that we used the method, the alarm went off only once—and just as Jay was reaching for it.

Rather proud of myself, I shared this method at a retreat. Afterward, a pastor's wife pulled me aside. "Sandra, your alarm clock method worked well for your family," she said, "but in ours it would never work. Our daughter would come home before curfew, turn off the alarm, and then go out again."

I had never considered that! I couldn't wait to get home and talk to my kids. Since the dinner hour was our favorite time to discuss heavy issues, I told them about the woman's comments at the retreat.

Then I said, "Now look, you both are young adults now, so I'm not going to hand out retroactive punishment. But I need to know: Did you ever come in just to turn off the alarm and then sneak out again?"

Both of them looked at me with wide eyes. In that moment, I knew two things: (1) They had never turned off the alarm to go out again; and (2) they were irritated it had never occurred to them.

An Encouraging Hug

Honey, your children need standards—including reasonable curfews.

85

Later Rewards

Pleasant words are a honeycomb, sweet to the soul and healing to the bones.

Proverbs 16:24

Children are indeed a blessing. And we parents have every reason to desire a close relationship with our offspring. Often, though, we remain ignorant of the barriers that hinder such closeness simply because we don't take time to get our children's input. So, right now, ask them what you are doing right and what you can improve. You might be surprised.

Even though my children had to be raised in a single-parent home, both have turned out to be fun, responsible adults. (Thank you, Lord!) Of the two, Jay continues to be the more reticent; Holly occasionally joins me in speaking at mother/daughter banquets. Her chosen theme is usually "Things My Mom Did Right—and What I Wish She Had Done Differently," so she has given me permission to include a few of her thoughts here. I hope it will be an encouragement to you too.

"I have a great time sharing the platform with Mom, especially since I get to encourage other mothers, telling them that the time they spend with their children is not wasted. Here are some of the things my mom has done right:

"She always has time for me. More than once I remember her stopping what she was working on and giving me her full attention when I needed to talk to her. Looking back, I know it must have been exhausting for her to listen to my problems when she had so many stresses and responsibilities at work, but she never made me feel unimportant. If something mattered to me, then it mattered to her.

"She cares about what's going on in my life. As a teen, I'd listen to some of my friends talk about the stuff they'd pull on their parents, and I'd think, *Boy, my mom would never let me get away with that. Somehow she'd find out, and I'd get nailed.* It really keeps you on the straight and narrow if you believe you'll get caught.

"She gives encouragement. And, boy, has that been a great help, especially during my college struggles. I thought I was going to die my freshman year when I had so many adjustments to make with new living arrangements and endless exams and papers. But my mom always gave me a fresh outlook on things and let me know I would survive.

"She's always ready with a hug. Even when I was little, she was a big one for hugs. Back then, I'd most likely be heading toward something she didn't want me to get into, so she'd say, 'Hurry, hurry! I need a hug.' And she'd hold out her arms to me.

"Well, I was just a toddler, and I didn't know what would happen if I didn't hurry and give her a hug. I mean, would she explode or something? So I'd rush to her arms and feel proud that once again I had stopped a possible explosion.

"Now, of course, there are a few things I wish my mom had done differently. For example, she still thinks she has to tell me how to drive! She'll say, 'Uh, honey, that light's red.' But that light is a mile away. I don't need to start braking while I'm still in the next county!

"But I love her, so I guess I'll keep putting up with her antics—just as she's been putting up with mine."

Ah, how good it is for a parent to be able to sigh with relief!

An Encouraging Hug

Honey, keep hanging in there. Rewards do come.

86

Happier Holidays

We who are strong ought to bear with the failings of the weak and not to please ourselves.

Romans 15:1

Looking for ways to de-stress the holidays? For years that was my goal as I found myself wondering, *How do I stop this runaway train we call Christmas?* Then I realized it was *my* hand on the throttle. As soon as I took a deep breath, lifted my hand off the emotional throttle, and asked my family what activities they found stressful about Christmas—so we could eliminate those traditions—we all began to enjoy the holiday and truly concentrate on the *spiritual* rather than the commercial celebration.

But it didn't take long for us to realize that what brought us comfort made others uncomfortable. For example, a couple of seasons ago, one of my friends asked in early December if I was ready for Christmas.

"Oh, yes," I replied.

"I just hate people like you," she said.

I chuckled. "Eva, it's easy to be ready for Christmas when you don't send cards, don't bake, and don't buy many gifts."

And that's true. Our family chose to be more interested in concentrating on family gatherings and remembering the reason for the holiday. Instead of sending Christmas cards, I try to send letters throughout the year. (By the way, with more than four hundred close personal friends and relatives on my list, I do resort to group letters for news about a move or important family events—adding a personal note at the bottom. And I enjoy the group letters that fill my mailbox each year—no matter what the advice columnists say.)

Instead of baking my former twelve different kinds of cookies these Kentucky hips don't need, I spend that time doing something special with friends. Instead of splurging on a zillion gifts for each other, my children and I often buy items for older folks, donating them through our local senior-citizens organization. One year I wrote to the relatives with whom we normally exchanged gifts, telling them instead of sending presents, we were planning henceforth to buy items in their name for some seniors in our area who didn't have family. Then I named the specific article we were giving that year—such as "Mary will receive the blue sweater she asked for." Other years I write a check to my favorite Appalachian mission. Instead of being upset, the relatives are relieved they don't have to buy gifts for us. One caution, though: Give the people on your list at least a couple of months notice about your decision. Some of my relatives start shopping in September!

An Encouraging Hug

Honey, look around your home. Do you really need one more thing to dust? So go ahead and de-stress the holidays.

87

The Contract

*Now if you obey me fully and keep my covenant, then out
of all nations you will be my treasured possession.*

Exodus 19:5

You know from your own experience that parenting isn't
easy. And if you're new to the adventure, let me assure
you the emotional work never ends. Sure, the physical
work lessens once we get past diapers and two o'clock
feedings, but it never gets easy.

But even in the midst of parental challenges, we are
to continue to pray, be diligent, and be creative. For
example, at the end of sixth grade and a few months after
Holly's twelfth birthday, she asked when she could start
dating. I was astounded by her question but managed
to reply calmly, "Well, when do you think would be a
good time to start?"

She thought for a moment, then said, "I think sixteen
is a good age."

I wasted no time. "That's a good idea, Holly. Why don't we write that down, along with a few other thoughts." So we dutifully drew up what would later be known as "The Contract." We sat at the dining table in our Michigan home and discussed several situations. Then she carefully printed the following rules in her twelve-year-old handwriting:

1. At fourteen and a half, the start of freshman year, a boy can come over to do homework—at the kitchen table.
2. At fifteen, a parent drives for group dates.
3. No "real" dates until sixteen. Curfew will be eleven o'clock, or a time agreed to by Mom and Holly.
4. No kissing until sixteen for Big Party of Holly's choice. (I explained that a "Sweet Sixteen" party meant she hadn't yet been kissed, so if Holly wanted to have this particular Big Party, she couldn't start kissing until after she turned sixteen.)
5. No going steady until college.
6. No getting engaged until Holly's senior year in college.
7. No marriage until Holly's college degree is completed.
8. Rules may be added to this list.

Holly wrote the date—May 13, 1986—at the top of the paper, and then we both signed it. I folded it and put it in a safe place.

Of course, during the next four years, she often regretted ever having created such rules for herself. When she'd insist that she be allowed to date before reaching the agreed-on age, I'd calmly ask, "What does The Contract say, Holly?"

She'd stomp out of the room, muttering, "I'm never signing anything again." Her friends didn't help much either. They told Holly she had signed something at twelve that had no relevance to the real world. They said I was being too strict with her. Ah, but The Contract provided a neutral buffer during the teen years. And now that Holly is well past that stage, she says she plans to have the same agreement with her children. Whew!

An Encouraging Hug

Honey, thinking ahead will save you aggravation later on.

88

Pray the Psalms

Call to me and I will answer you and tell you great and unsearchable things you do not know.

Jeremiah 33:3

Every parent, at one time or another, worries about the path lying before a beloved child. Many of these parents find it helpful to use the Psalms as a foundation for prayer. As an example, here's a prayer based on Psalm 25:16–21: *Lord, turn to* (insert child's name) *and be gracious to him, for he is lonely and afflicted. The troubles of his heart have multiplied; free him from his anguish. Look upon his affliction and his distress and take away all his sins. See how his enemies have increased and how fiercely they hate him! Guard his life and rescue him; let him not be put to shame, for he takes refuge in you. May integrity and uprightness protect him, because his hope is in you.*

During her son's teen years, Karen keeps reminding God of Clayton and asks him to protect her boy and love him and gently bring him back into the fold. She confesses the word *gently* may be a problem as she wonders if God will lovingly bring him back or take him through the deepest pain to jerk him back.

One of my friends got to the point with her son that she finally prayed, "Whatever it takes, Lord. If it costs an arm or a leg or an eye, whatever it takes, bring him back to you."

Many of us want to pray that prayer, but we're afraid to—and afraid not to. I once believed I could create a perfect personal world if I just worked hard enough at it. Now I understand my goal is to work hard at turning impossible situations over to the Lord. He alone can give us the internal peace we long for. He alone can help us rest in him. The problem is, of course, we want our children to know the richness of God's peace and power, but we don't want them to have to go through the painful process. Let's remind ourselves that the heavenly Father is shaping those we love, not destroying them, and allowing them to go through their turmoil is part of his training.

An Encouraging Hug

Honey, pray the Psalms over your children—before they make wrong choices.

89

Be Involved

But just as he who called you is holy, so be holy in all you do; for it is written: "Be holy, because I am holy."

1 Peter 1:15–16

The contract Holly had written at age twelve got us safely past her sixteenth birthday. Then, after our move to Colorado Springs, young wrestlers with necks like tree trunks appeared on my doorstep, asking to date my beautiful daughter.

It was time for "The Talk." This conversation consisted of Holly's would-be date having to answer a series of questions about his interests, previous residences, and family background. Of course that was *supposed* to be my husband's role, but there was no one but me to follow through on it. And follow through I did!

One young man was nervous and kept glancing toward the stairway, wondering when Holly would be ready.

I smiled. "It's okay. She'll be down when this is over."

I gestured toward the window where I could see his blue car parked in front of the house. I uttered the challenge of a concerned parent: "That's a nice car. Obviously you take good care of it. But what would you do if a stranger came to your door one evening and asked if he could borrow it, even if he said he'd take good care of it?"

The lad smiled in sudden understanding. "I'd tell him I'd have to get to know him first."

I nodded. "Exactly. You've shown up here asking to take my daughter out for the evening. She is far more precious to me than your car is to you. I didn't know anything about you before we began this talk. Right now you think this is ridiculous, but I guarantee in about twenty years when a stranger comes to your door to borrow your daughter for the evening, you'll think of me and say, 'That ol' lady was right!'"

I let that thought sink in. Then I continued. "Another thing: You two are just going out as friends, but I've lived long enough to know how quickly situations can change. So remember this: Treat Holly the way you hope some other guy is treating *your* future wife."

His eyes widened. I knew I'd hit my target and won the round.

Word got around. Whenever a new guy hinted he'd like to ask Holly out, the other guys would warn him about The Talk. One classmate told Holly he hoped I hadn't changed my mind, saying, "I had to go through it; I want him to have to face your mom too."

Only one young man refused to meet with me, saying, "That's ridiculous! This isn't the 1800s!" Holly told him not to call her again. "It's like my mom says, 'You don't have to like it; you just have to do it,'" she said.

And, yes, I had Jay's dates over for lunch to meet them before they went out together. But I confess I didn't make them sweat in the same way I did those young wrestlers!

An Encouraging Hug

Honey, be involved in your teen's dating.

90

Decision Making

Whether you turn to the right or to the left, your ears will hear a voice behind you, saying, "This is the way; walk in it."

Isaiah 30:21

We've all heard the saying "A decision not made is a decision in itself." However, those of us who don't like change would prefer to ignore the problem rather than decide what the right choice is. And of course good choices often remain unmade because we are afraid we will make the wrong one.

Here are a few thoughts if you have to make a decision.

Start with prayer. The Lord encourages us to bring every problem to him. A woman once asked G. Campbell Morgan, the great preacher, if she should take everything to the Lord or just the big things. Morgan laughed as he assured her, "Take everything to him. After all, what could you possibly present to God that would be *big* to him?"

After we pray, though, we have some definite steps to take.

Ask yourself if you are delaying this decision because you are afraid of change. If so, determine not to let fear decide your future. Then state aloud or write down what outcome you want. Sometimes just identifying your objectives clearly will help you make a better decision. Don't limit yourself—or allow others to limit you—with the thought, *But I've never done that before.*

Gather information about potential results. If possible, have a trial run. I remember friends in our Sunday school class who were determined they were going to make vacations easier by buying a motor home. A mutual friend listened to the father's expectations of what this expensive vehicle would provide for his family and quietly suggested they rent one first. The father assured him that would be a waste of money since the $350 rental fee would make a nice down payment toward the purchase. Our friend still quietly insisted. Good thing he did. That rental trip revealed that vacationing with five children in a motor home did not live up to the father's fantasy.

Trust your "gut." When I state my new decision aloud after I've prayed, I pay attention to how my stomach reacts. If it hurts, I know I'd better not follow through on it. Others may experience some other physical manifestation—rapidly beating heart, shortness of breath, weak knees—that may indicate that they shouldn't proceed.

Go forth in confidence. A few years ago I was concerned about the decision I had made over the sale of some furniture, so I confided in Morrie, a family friend. In his typical Dutch way, he said gently, "You've made your decision; now live with it."

In my decision-making process, I do two additional things: First, I take a long walk in an old cemetery to remind me that if this decision doesn't have eternal results, it really doesn't matter. Second, I ask myself, *A year from now, what are you going to wish you had done?* The two times I've asked myself that question, cross-country moves resulted as I answered, *I will wish I had had the courage to accept the new career opportunities the Lord was offering.*

Sure, neither move turned out exactly the way I had hoped, but my children and I wouldn't have missed either move for the world. And along the way, all of us learned important lessons.

An Encouraging Hug

Honey, take a deep breath and make that decision.

91

Empty Nesting

And this is my prayer: that your love may abound more
and more in knowledge and depth of insight.

Philippians 1:9

The middle-aged couple was on their way home from
their youngest child's wedding. Suddenly the wife began
to cry. "Now it's just the two of us," she said.

Her husband glanced at her and said quietly, "That's
the way we started out."

The term *empty nest* may sound ominous, but, if we've
done our job well, that's exactly what we're supposed
to end up with. It doesn't mean the end of our family.
It just means we're entering a time when we relate to
each other more as adult friends than as parents and
children.

Now that my children are grown, friends often ask
if I'm upset about having entered the empty-nest stage.
My flippant reply is more for myself than for them: "If

there's anything worse than adult children leaving home, it's adult children *not* leaving home."

Some of my friends add even more reality and say that what's worse than their leaving is their coming *back* after they've been away. Author Patsy Clairmont says she always knew her children would grow up and move out, but she didn't realize they would multiply and come back!

So accept this time as a new adventure. Wonderful days are still ahead.

An Encouraging Hug

Honey, the empty nest isn't the end of your life. It's the start of a new one.

92

Letting Go

Honor your father and your mother, so that you may live long in the land the LORD your God is giving you.

Exodus 20:12

The hardest part of my children growing up was my realization that I was no longer in control. When they were little, I knew where they were—usually underfoot. Suddenly, I knew only where they were *supposed* to be. But I didn't want to be like the mother in the silly movie *Throw Mama from the Train,* who was always treating her middle-aged son, Owen, as though he were still eight years old. In fact, when I caught myself ordering college student Jay around, I'd shriek in my best weird-mother voice, "Owen! Owen!" to remind myself that my new role was to be an encourager and mentor. Jay, of course, just grinned at my silliness.

I also didn't want to be like the ninety-year-old mother of one of the women who attended a writer's conference where I spoke. By the second day of the conference, the mother had called her daughter saying she had no business being at the conference, she would never be a writer, and she should come home immediately. The attendee was seventy years old!

Another instructor and I talked with her and prayed with her, but nothing we said could change her belief that she still had to obey her mother. When Exodus 20:12 says, "Honor your father and your mother," it means exactly that—honor, respect, encourage, help— not sacrifice your very being for your parents' every whim.

I also don't want to be like one of my cousins who not only expects her children to visit her every Sunday afternoon but also insists they spend every holiday at her house. I'm amazed she refuses to see that perhaps, just perhaps, her children have (or should have!) a life of their own.

An Encouraging Hug

Honey, learn from these examples as you allow your adult children to have a life outside of your control.

93

Practice Runs

Be self-controlled and alert. Your enemy the devil prowls around like a roaring lion looking for someone to devour.

1 Peter 5:8

What helps parents get ready for the empty nest? Letting go in little spurts.

Years ago, when I was an editor in New York, I had the privilege of interviewing Jay Kesler, then president of Taylor University in Upland, Indiana. As we talked about children leaving home, he said, "The wrens that have a nest in our yard don't wait until the cat is there to decide to give their little ones the acid test. They start by letting the babes take little loops around the nest. When they're able to fly well, they fly away. This is what we're to do as parents. We teach our children to take these ever enlarging loops until they can leave the nest."

So give your children experiences in responsibility. Staying overnight with Grandma or with trusted families is a good start. Later, handling money—even doing the math in the parent's checkbook for a couple of months—and caring for pets helps too. If children have not had any responsibility for maintaining their room or handling money before they leave home, they may not have success when they are on their own.

Kesler agreed, "The truth is, independence has not been built into them. Young people need to be increasingly trusted with responsibilities—such as using the family car. But you don't do that in one big gulp overnight. You start it when they're small. Occasionally those little loops will include mistakes, such as spending money foolishly. But if they aren't given that opportunity when they're young, they'll have to learn that lesson in adulthood when their whole family will suffer."

So keeping in mind Dr. Kesler's wise words, start giving your young person little spurts of ever increasing responsibility.

An Encouraging Hug

Honey, letting go is a stretching time for the entire family.

94

Thank-You Notes

Give thanks to the LORD, for he is good; his love endures forever.

Psalm 107:1

Taking the time to write a thank-you note is time consuming and stress producing—especially if we're the parent trying to get the kids to write the note. Many of my friends have the simple rule that the item cannot be used or the money spent until the thank-you note is written. But what do you do if the gift is not one the child is looking forward to using? This is where we need to remember that we are the parent as we insist that appreciation be expressed.

Sometimes it's enough to remind the child that if someone went to the trouble to think of him or her by choosing a gift, even if he or she doesn't appreciate the gift, the child must express appreciation for the thoughtfulness shown.

One young mother always tells her children that if they have enough time to unwrap a gift, they have enough time to write a brief note. She also keeps a good supply of thank-you cards and stamps on hand as birthdays and holidays approach so no excuses can be offered.

Yes, it can be exhausting to make sure our children learn to express appreciation, but we have an excellent example of the importance of thankfulness in Luke 17:11–19. This is the story of the ten lepers who called out for Jesus to have pity on their condition. Jesus responded by telling them to go and show themselves to the priest (v. 14). "And as they went"—as they were in the process of obeying—"they were cleansed." Verse 15 says that only one of the ten came back to thank Jesus. In verse 17 Jesus asks, "Were not all ten cleansed? Where are the other nine?"

Yes, a thank-you is important indeed.

An Encouraging Hug

Honey, yes, it takes time—and patience—to encourage note writing, but expressions of appreciation are important.

95

Scripture Puzzles

I have hidden your word in my heart that I might not sin against you.

Psalm 119:11

When I was in vacation Bible school as a child, we were correctly taught that memorizing Scripture would help keep us from sin. In the decades since then, I have had more than a few opportunities to prove that it's true. One corporate friend said that when he's tempted to pad an expense report, "Thou shalt not steal" comes to mind immediately. I've also learned that memorizing Scripture gets us through tough times when we can't read our Bibles.

A few years ago I met Daniel, a Chinese citizen who had been imprisoned for sharing his faith in his homeland. He described the long hours that stretched into days then weeks then months, when none of the dozen men in his cell was allowed to move or speak from after breakfast until supper—except for the cell leader, who paced before them, lecturing on the evils they had committed. Daniel said he kept his head down and alternated between silently praying and quoting every hymn and Scripture verse he could remember. That's how he survived the eight months.

In a lecture series, a local financial brokerage firm recently featured a retired Air Force colonel who had been imprisoned in Vietnam. As he described his ordeal, he explained the wall-tapping code with which he and the other isolated prisoners communicated. Their tapping kept them in touch with each other and sane as they passed along poems, words to songs, and Bible verses.

In my own life, when I was taking care of my dying husband and didn't have chunks of time to read Scripture, I had to pull on the strength from the verses I had stored in my mind years before.

So get the Word into your children's minds. Not only for the challenges they face now but for the ones that will be ahead. To make Scripture memorization fun, one mother prints the Scripture in large letters on the computer, then makes a jigsaw puzzle out of them. Another mother quizzes her children at each meal by repeating the verse but pausing every few words for her children to fill in the blanks. Use whatever memorization method works for your family. It will pay off. What we learn in childhood stays with us.

An Encouraging Hug

Honey, find a way to put the Scriptures into the heads and hearts of your children now.

96

Teachable Moments

As for me, far be it from me that I should sin against the LORD *by failing to pray for you. And I will teach you the way that is good and right.*

1 Samuel 12:23

Rich and Elizabeth Blanco of Colorado Springs are like many other parents—watching for those teachable moments that allow them not only to expand their young children's minds but to instruct them about Jesus.

Elizabeth says, *"Every* moment is a teachable moment," as she and Rich parent their young daughters, Kayleigh and Hannah—protecting and loving them, teaching them about faith, helping them accept the consequences of their actions, and answering questions about everything around them.

Elizabeth's favorite time of the day is when she is cuddled with each daughter as they talk about their day and read a bedtime story together. "I love lying next to them and reading," she says. "They feel secure and know they can talk about anything. And I love the unexpected 'I love you' and sudden kisses."

She continues: "And I like being there for them—whether it's comforting them when they wake up because of a scary dream or cooking their favorite meals."

Rich is also involved in the children's day-to-day activities, including playing sports with them and explaining new concepts. Recently Kayleigh, having heard a TV commercial use the word *calorie*, asked what that is. Rich thought for a moment, considered her age, and then explained, "It's the fuel for our bodies that's found in food. Just as putting gasoline in our car tank gives it energy to take us places, so eating the right kinds of food gives us energy too."

At another time Rich's availability led to his leading both girls to the Lord during a discussion about heaven. In fact Hannah was only three and a half years old when she said heaven sounded pretty and that she wanted to go there someday.

Rich wondered if perhaps she wasn't too young to understand spiritual concepts, but he didn't want to let the moment pass. "Well, the only way you can go to heaven is if you ask Jesus to come and live in your heart," he said.

Then, as he explained in three-year-old terms what that meant, Hannah smiled and said, "I want to do that!"

Since then, Rich and Elizabeth have continued to talk about what it means to have Jesus in their lives, and both girls have the concept—and the faith—down pat. And it all happened because a parent was ready for those teachable moments.

An Encouraging Hug

Honey, watch for those times that allow you to instruct
your children about their world and share with them the
Lord's reality.

97

Talking to a Child about Death or Divorce

Peace I leave with you; my peace I give you. I do not give to you as the world gives. Do not let your hearts be troubled and do not be afraid.

John 14:27

Death and divorce are two of life's traumas we wish we'd never have to discuss. But if you do, here are a few suggestions.

Be truthful. Many times, a parent, thinking the truth is too stark for the child, gives an unhealthy, false explanation, such as "Grandma's gone on a long trip," or "Daddy had to leave on business." Not only are these lies, but they postpone having to tell the truth that the grandmother has died or the father has walked out. Meanwhile, the child may feel resentful because the special person left without saying good-bye. Be aware that if the missing person hasn't said good-bye, the child will feel abandoned.

Tell only what the child can handle. While it's imperative we be truthful, it is not necessary to give children all the gory details. I initially spared my children the details of their dad's death, telling them only that his brain cancer produced a blood clot that hit his lungs and he died. Almost three years later, Jay asked if his dad had been in a lot of pain. I quoted the doctor, who said a pulmonary embolism is just like having the lights go out. I don't know if it's true, but I take comfort in it. I was with Don when the clot hit his lungs, so I know that even if the pain was intense, death came quickly. That's all I could tell Jay. And that was enough, since it settled his mind on the issue.

In the case of divorce, you don't need to tell the ugly details, such as your spouse's adultery, but you need to answer the child's questions. A terse "I don't want to talk about it" puts up walls a child cannot scale. In response, the child will withdraw, often with sad results.

Encourage children to express feelings. Some parents are so afraid of emotion they insist their children suppress it too. But children who are allowed to express emotion not only fare better at the time but develop stronger patterns for coping with stress later.

Don't assume. Margaret Bole's mother died when Margaret was only four. Her father took her and her siblings to their grandmother's, saying he'd be back for them. "Of course he never came back," she says. But every night, she would line up her little shoes by the door. Then she'd lie flat on her back and fluff her hair just so, lying stiffly so she wouldn't muss it in case he came for her in the night.

"We never know what is in the heart of children," she says.

Pamela would agree. When she and her husband divorced, they assumed their son was "handling" it well since he didn't cry or ask questions. In reality, he was teeming with questions and self-accusations that later manifested themselves through discipline problems at school.

Understand guilt. The child often wonders if he or she caused the death or the divorce, especially if there was tension between the child and the parent.

In an interview, former first lady Rosalynn Carter said she was thirteen when her father died of leukemia. She added, "For many years, I had a very guilty conscience because I thought I was partly to blame for his sickness and death."

Pete remembers his dad always telling him to play quietly. Even as an adult, Pete wonders if his dad would have stayed with the family if he had been less boisterous.

Make sure your child doesn't lose you too. Too often the remaining parent's grief causes the child to lose the second parent emotionally. Early in her widowhood, Glenna found herself wondering if she had fed the children breakfast before they left for school one morning. It was only when she saw the three cereal bowls in the sink that she knew she had.

That evening, she talked to the children about how much she missed their daddy, stopping occasionally to wipe away tears. Her nine-year-old son, Frank, nodded sadly. "It's like you aren't here either."

Only then did Glenna understand how frightened her children had been as they watched her grieve. In that moment, she determined she needed to talk to the children, sharing memories and asking for theirs as well. She also stopped retreating to her bedroom when she felt the tears welling up. Instead, she would wrap her arms around the closest child and say, "I need a hug."

This openness is just as important for divorced parents. The remaining parent may hide behind an emotional wall, not realizing that pushing the pain down will only cause it to seep out in some other way, often through inappropriate anger or destructive eating or drinking habits. What helps during this time too is for the parent to talk to adults who have weathered similar storms.

Let the child talk. Whether the loss is through death or divorce, let the child talk about it, sharing his or her special memories and sense of loss.

Encourage communication. Lack of verbalization doesn't mean lack of questions, so try to get kids talking. Ask if they have specific concerns. Share how you felt when you were their age and were faced with similar situations.

Affirm the child's feelings. When a child feels anything but sadness, the most common reaction is for the adult to say, "Don't feel like that!" Normal emotions may include anger—even at the deceased parent or the one most wronged in the divorce. An adult's negative response adds greater turmoil to the child's emotions. Feelings aren't conjured up by the child—they just *are.*

And here's a suggestion for those who know a suffering family: Be there for them. Don't say you will be there and then conveniently forget when the emotion of the funeral or divorce proceedings are past.

Helping take up some of the parenting slack is where the church can make a major difference in a child's life. I'm not suggesting *one* man or woman absorb all of the responsibility, but if several deacons or the missing parent's friends would include the child even once a month with his or her own family, it would make a marvelous difference in that young life.

An Encouraging Hug

Honey, talking with and listening to children during these times not only acknowledges their grief but also affirms their importance within the family.

98

One Family's Courage

Let us then approach the throne of grace with confidence,
so that we may receive mercy and find grace to help us in
our time of need.

Hebrews 4:16

Leslie and Tom Kaluzny of Washington State are the
parents of six children. A few years ago their youngest,
one-year-old Jeremiah, was diagnosed with an inoper-
able brain tumor. The only symptom that had sent him
into the two-week round of tests was an ongoing loss
of weight.

When Leslie and Jeremiah returned from the hospital,
the children had to cope with not only the sight of their
baby brother being hooked up to an IV but also having
their family schedule totally altered. And the shadow
of the tumor hung over them all—especially with the
doctor's prognosis that Jeremiah would become blind
and increasingly less mobile as the tumor advanced.

Even their evenings were different. In the past, the time just before going to bed was a peaceful winding down of the day's activities. They'd all gather in one large bedroom to sing, read the Word, and pray. Suddenly Leslie and Jeremiah couldn't be part of this time since she had to rock him to sleep so he wouldn't pull out the IV lines.

Amazing as it may seem, the other children weren't resentful of the special attention Jeremiah received, but they were fearful of the outcome. Micah, the then eleven-year-old, found it especially difficult to talk about his little brother as he wondered why this had happened to his family, but he also felt they were actually closer since they didn't know what was going to happen. He also saw the effect this sweet baby had on people in their community, and he listened to his parents pray that Jeremiah's impact on the body of Christ would be great. He watched, pondering the events and the possible outcome, and he had to deal with his bewilderment—and anger—that God was saying no to their prayers for healing.

Leslie says, "As parents, Tom and I were utterly dependent on God to reveal to our children what he was doing—and why—since we couldn't answer all of their questions. The children saw that Jeremiah's life affected others. People we didn't even know were praying for him. But we couldn't make our children trust God more. We could only trust that those critical heart issues would make them grow strong in their faith, building character to help them walk uprightly before him. We couldn't make those changes in them."

Sadly, Jeremiah died a year and a half after the diagnosis.

When Catherine Marshall was widowed, she took to her bed after Peter's funeral. As her mother sat with her, Catherine asked the eternal question: "Why?"

Her mother, also a widow, answered quietly, "In God's time, he will give you *his* answer."

And that's all any of us can hope for as we try to understand why God allows grief into our lives.

An Encouraging Hug

Honey, our choice is not *whether* we will go through tough times but *how*.

99

An Important Apology

Fathers, do not exasperate your children; instead, bring
them up in the training and instruction of the Lord.

Ephesians 6:4

Do you owe someone an apology?

Saying "I'm sorry" *is* difficult. We'd rather blame our
sharp words or cruel actions on stress or even the other
person. But the situation won't be right until we *make*
it right.

I remember a long-ago radio preacher telling a story.
I've forgotten his name, but the story is one to which we
can all relate. In the late 1400s some young boys were
watching the famous Leonardo da Vinci paint *The Last*
Supper on a wall of a Milano monastery. One of them
backed up to get a better look—and knocked over a stack
of canvases. The artist was furious. Until that moment,
he had hardly known the boys were there as he intently
worked on the face of Jesus. Now, his concentration
broken, he threw his brush and yelled harsh words at

the frightened lad, who ran crying from the hall. The other boys quickly followed.

The artist was alone again and free to concentrate on his work, but the brush felt heavy in his fingers and the strokes were better suited for the painting of the table than the peaceful features of the Lord announcing the one who would betray him. Da Vinci's creativity had stopped.

Finally, he put down his brush and left the hall. He walked for several hours until he found the little boy who had been in his studio. Stooping before him, da Vinci said, "I'm sorry, child. I shouldn't have spoken so hastily."

Then taking the lad's hand, he escorted him back into the hall and picked up the brush. Only then did the face of Jesus appear—a face that, I'm convinced, could not have been produced if the artist had not apologized.

What good things are waiting to be released in our lives by those simple words "I'm sorry"?

An Encouraging Hug

Honey, I know it is difficult, but sometimes the most important two words are "I'm sorry."

100

Bragging Rights

Pride goes before destruction, a haughty spirit before a fall.

Proverbs 16:18

One of our military friends, Joe, couldn't wait to tell his family he had been promoted from captain to major. When he walked through the back door, his seven-year-old daughter, Betsy, was at the kitchen table coloring. As she looked up to greet him, he said, "Betsy, guess what I became today?"

She took one look at his face and squealed, "You're president of the United States?"

How do you confess you're only a major after that?

Children have a wonderful way of putting accomplishments into the proper perspective—and for showing us how we appear to others.

Before Jay and Holly started driving, many of our adventures included my getting lost—and my absent-mindedly going *in* the *out* side of the parking lot. They groaned with each misadventure, but once they began to share in the driving responsibilities, they understood how easy it is to get lost in new territory and that faded yellow arrows in the parking lot can easily lead to confusion. Then, just as college graduation loomed, we had dinner with our friend Matt, whose father is president of a large Detroit funeral home chain. It was my turn to drive, so in my usual forgetful style, I exited through the *in* lane of the restaurant parking lot.

When my passengers stopped teasing me, Jay turned to Matt and said, "When we have to bury Mom, I want your dad to instruct the driver to go *in* the *out* lane of the cemetery—just for old time's sake."

And we all laughed.

Just as Joe, who had not become president of the United States that day, chose to see the humor in his daughter's joyful assumption, I chose to laugh at my children's teasing. And I hope they someday *do* follow through on their threatened suggestion to Matt's dad.

An Encouraging Hug

Honey, take your parenting responsibilities seriously but never yourself.

101

A Bowl of Oatmeal

Let the peace of Christ rule in your hearts, since as members of one body you were called to peace. And be thankful.

Colossians 3:15

In any family, an important attribute is a good attitude. Whenever I mention the word *attitude*, I always think of an experience my friend Lanson Ross had when he was growing up.

Lanson said his mother was not the best cook in the world. And as proof of that, every morning she made the same thing for breakfast—oatmeal. She would boil the water, throw in the oats, and throw in the salt, and then she would *never* stir it. So when Lanson went downstairs to breakfast, he didn't know if he was going to get the top part that was all raw, the side part that was all salt, or the bottom part that was all burned. He just knew he was going to get a bowl of *bad* oatmeal.

One morning Lanson was particularly hungry and particularly irritated, knowing what was waiting downstairs. And this was before the days of being able to stop at the fast food place on the corner and get a sausage biscuit. If you were a growing boy and hungry, you ate what was waiting downstairs.

Lanson shared a room with his younger brother, who was one of those cheerful morning guys. You know the type—one who tap-dances and whistles while he's buttoning his shirt. Normally Lanson would ignore him, but this morning Lanson was hungry and irritated.

So he turned to his brother and snarled, "How can you be so cheerful every morning? Don't you know we're going downstairs to the same bad oatmeal?"

His brother turned to him in surprise. "Oh, no, Lanson," he said. "It's never the same. Why, you don't know if you're going to get the raw part or the salty part or the burned part. But it's never the same."

Same situation; different responses. And all because of attitude.

An Encouraging Hug

Honey, at one time or another, life hands all of us repeated bowls of bad oatmeal. Our attitude will make the difference in how we respond.

To Ponder and Discuss

1. As Different as Night and Day

1. What evidence can you cite from your own family to support the idea that children have—or don't have—definite prebirth personalities?
2. What examples do you have of your children being as different as night and day?

2. Just Who Was Lost Again?

1. What frantic moments have your children given you?
2. If you had it to do over, what changes would you make for safety?

3. Shopping Cart Adventures

1. What challenges do you face when you go shopping with your children?
2. What have you found to be helpful while you are in the grocery aisles?

4. Cleaning Ladies Are Biblical

1. What is the biggest challenge in your schedule?

2. What attributes of the Proverbs 31 Woman would you like to claim?

5. Wishing Away Today

1. Have you ever found yourself wishing away this stage? If so, what was the situation?
2. How do you try to appreciate the gift of each new day?

6. Cooling Off

1. Have you ever gone beyond what was necessary to impress company? Care to explain the situation?
2. Most parents have a "naked child" story. What's yours?

7. The Pretty Jungle

1. Have you ever needlessly hurried your children? If so, what was the result?
2. Have your children taught you to slow down a bit?

8. A Little Buddy

1. What special memories do you carry in your heart?
2. What experiences would you like to do over?

9. Looking Ahead

1. In what ways did your life change once you became a parent?
2. In what ways were you surprised by your new responsibilities?

10. Joyful Laughter

1. What question has your child asked that opened your eyes to a particular situation?

2. Do you try to put more humor into your family's day? Why or why not?

11. A New Vocabulary

1. What are some of the fun expressions your family uses?
2. What do you think of the college professor's insistence that only proper English be used with children?

12. Peaceful Sleep

1. What unusual ways have your children found to awaken you?
2. Do you agree or disagree that sleep deprivation is a problem for parents of young children?

13. Milestone Days

1. What was the biggest surprise you had in your schedule once you became a parent?
2. What do you think about the 1930s community that took over all of the chores for the new mother?

14. Veteran Wisdom

1. In what ways do you allow your children to use their imagination?
2. What do you find nurtures the spirits of your family members?

15. Eyeball Listening

1. What habits have you changed to the benefit of your family?
2. What have you learned from your children when you've taken the time to listen?

16. Fun Memories

1. What are some of the things your family does for fun?
2. What is a fun experience your children will remember for a long time?

17. New Taste

1. How do you get your children to try new things?
2. To which experiences could your family reply, "Well, we can cross that off our list"?

18. Encouraging Humor

1. How do you use humor to lighten a tense moment?
2. How do you encourage your children to get their chores done?

19. Little Acts, Big Results

1. Have you ever witnessed a neighborhood feud that started between children? If so, what happened?
2. Have you ever been tempted to become involved in your child's squabbles? If so, care to share the situation?

20. Welcoming a Different Personality

1. In what ways do you try to allow your children to be who they are rather than who you want them to be?
2. Have you ever purchased a gift for your child because it was something you always wanted? If so, what was it?

21. The Dinner Hour

1. Describe the seating arrangement at your dinner table.
2. How often does your schedule allow your family to have dinner together?

22. Tangible Care

1. Do you have a family verse? Why did you select that particular one?
2. What changes would you like to make in the area of family communication?

23. A Morning Blessing

1. Would a morning blessing work with your family's schedule? Why or why not?
2. In what ways do you pray for your children throughout the day?

24. Simple Reminders

1. In what little ways do you try to remind your children of your love?
2. Have you ever been surprised by your child's invitation to share his or her school day with you?

25. Scary Moments

1. Can you identify with Diane's frantic reaction? Why or why not?
2. What advice do you have for parents who think about leaving their children alone for a few minutes?

26. Home Alone

1. What precautions have you taken should your child get home before you do?

2. What suggestions do you have for parents of latch-key children?

27. A Favorite Photo

1. What is your favorite family photo?
2. If a photo were to capture the personality of each family member, what would it show?

28. A "Cookie Baker," Anyone?

1. What do you think about the "cookie baker" idea for kids who think they're too old for baby-sitters?
2. What are your thoughts on security systems?

29. Add Some Joy

1. Do you agree that the parent's outlook on life affects the child? Why or why not?
2. Describe what it means to rejoice in the Lord always.

30. Read to Your Babies

1. What good habits have you tried to establish with your children?
2. What are your thoughts on reciting nursery rhymes?

31. Special Company

1. Do you ever find that you get the house in shape faster when you're expecting company?
2. What do you think about Bea and Jack's plan to treat their children like company?

32. What Do You Want?

1. Do you identify in any way with Clara's saying her mother didn't know what would make her happy?

2. Do you know people who try to fill the hole in their heart with things?

33. Heaven Is Not Here

1. Have you ever been forced to learn that heaven is not here?
2. Which of the Lord's promises do you especially take to heart?

34. Take Charge

1. How do you feel about mothers working outside the home?
2. What suggestions do you have for companies that want to meet the needs of parents?

35. Memory Stones

1. What item do you have in your home that brings back memories of a special day?
2. What displayed item causes your guests to raise their eyebrows?

36. Creating Good Memories

1. How do you attempt to create good memories for your children?
2. What memory do you think your children would list as their favorite?

37. Encouraging Chitchat

1. What are some of the questions you ask to get your children to open up?
2. Where are some of the places your children are comfortable talking?

38. Opening Your Home

1. What is your reaction to the mother who put a blue ribbon across her living room doorway to keep her teens and their friends out?
2. In what ways do you attempt to open your home to your child's friends?

39. More Warm Welcomes

1. Has your child's choice of friends ever given you pause? If so, how did you handle the situation?
2. What is your greatest hospitality challenge?

40. Start When They're Small

1. What "finger chores" do you require of your children each day?
2. How do you try to be open to the unexpected?

41. A Missed Opportunity

1. Have you ever missed a "rainbow moment" with your child? If so, what happened?
2. Have you ever gotten a second chance at a missed opportunity? If so, what was the situation?

42. Stinging Words

1. What stinging words do you wish weren't part of your memory bank?
2. What helps you not pass along those same hurtful words to your children?

43. Old Tapes

1. How have you eased the effect of old mental tapes in your life?
2. In what ways do you try to encourage your children?

44. The Hippopotamus

1. About what situation do you wish you could have given your children more information?
2. Does your child have a special item that makes him or her more comfortable in new situations? If so, what is it?

45. Immediate Action

1. How do you attempt to direct your child's actions?
2. Have you ever asked your child, "What do you think you need from me?" What was the response?

46. Phone Hugs

1. Do you agree with the observation of "Little children, little problems. Big children, big problems"? Why or why not?
2. What do you think about phone hugs?

47. Little Ears

1. In what ways do you try to be careful of what you say in the presence of your child?
2. What is your reaction to the woman who said, "One has to do her duty" when speaking about caring for her grandchildren?

48. Early Lessons

1. Do you know folks whose childhood was influenced by the three rules: Don't talk, don't trust, don't feel?
2. In what ways are you attempting not to repeat your parents' mistakes?

49. Solid Direction

1. Can you remember an incident when you acted or spoke in a way that set a poor example for your children?
2. Do you agree that "values are more caught than taught"?

50. Good Examples

1. What helps you be aware of the example you are to your children?
2. Which of your examples would you like your children to pass on to their future children?

51. Not Wrong, Just Different

1. Have you ever been in a worship service that was very different from what you were used to? If so, care to describe the situation?
2. Why do you think Jesus performed his miracles in different ways?

52. Forgiveness

1. Do you agree forgiveness is one of the toughest principles for parents to teach their children? Why or why not?
2. Care to share any ways in which you have dealt with forgiveness in your own family?

53. Consider the Child

1. In what ways do you trust your instincts when it comes to your child's potential?
2. What do you think of the interpretation of the first part of Proverbs 22:6 as "Train a child in *his* way"?

54. Wise Choices

1. Do you agree with the saying "Youth is wasted on the young"? Why or why not?
2. Do you miss anything about your youth? If so, what?

55. Creative Strength

1. Have you ever had to go to a Plan B for those times when your first choice didn't work out? If so, care to share the situation?
2. Have you ever instructed your children to borrow your strength until they could muster their own? If so, care to share the situation?

56. Telling Stories

1. Do you tell family stories? If so, how? If not, would you like to begin?
2. Has an older relative or friend passed along a story that intrigued your children?

57. More Stories

1. Why do you think Jesus told stories?
2. Are you comfortable with your ability to tell a story? Why or why not?

58. God's Provision

1. Do you ever wish God would run his plans by you first?
2. In what ways have you learned that God is God and you're not?

59. Children's Prayers

1. Has your child's prayer ever gotten you out of a bad situation? If so, care to share?

2. Why do you think Jesus said adults should be more like children?

60. Tangible Reminders

1. In what ways does your home reflect who you are?
2. Do you have any family photos that have a funny story behind them? Care to share?

61. Passing the Baton

1. What stories do you hope your children will some-day be telling their children?
2. What's the toughest—and best—Christmas your family has experienced?

62. Typical Arguments

1. When are your children most prone to argue?
2. What rules would you suggest for parents whose children argue?

63. Odd and Even

1. Would the "odd and even" system work in your situation? Why or why not?
2. What is the most creative you've ever gotten in solving an argument?

64. Praying for Strangers

1. Have you ever had an opportunity to pray for a stranger? If so, what was the situation?
2. What visual or audible reminders do you use as a call to prayer?

65. Special Time

1. In what ways do you try to give each child special time?

2. How do you try to help your children appropriately express what they are feeling?

66. Practicing for the Future

1. What do you think of the idea of having older children see their kindnesses to each other as practice for future marriage?
2. What opportunities have you had to see your parenting bear good fruit?

67. Volunteer Workers

1. What has worked for you as you attempt to keep your children from developing a materialistic attitude?
2. Have you ever done volunteer work as a family? If so, what was the result?

68. Look around You

1. In what ways does your family try to reach out to your neighborhood?
2. Do you agree that one individual can make a big difference in this world? Why or why not?

69. A Spare Bed

1. Have you ever taken in your child's friend? If so, what happened?
2. In what ways have you stretched your spiritual muscles as you have tried to follow God's Word?

70. A Hand to Wave

1. How do you react to the school principal who asked church members to wave at designated children?

2. Do you agree that "if the church doesn't get involved in the lives of hurting children, we will lose an entire generation"? Why or why not?

71. Easing a Child's Stress

1. Do you think stress has increased in modern times? Why or why not?
2. In what ways do you try to ease your children's stress?

72. The Three Cs

1. Do you agree that in an addict's family the sick one controls the well ones? Why or why not?
2. In what ways do you think the family of the addict might be encouraged by the thought that they didn't cause the addiction, they can't control it, and they can't cure it?

73. Stress Relievers

1. What ways have you found to help relieve the stress in your family?
2. In what areas are you still working to relieve stress?

74. Signs of Stress

1. In what ways do you try to be aware of stress in your child's life?
2. What have you found to be helpful in easing childhood stress?

75. Dump the Guilt

1. Do you identify with any of the three types of guilt—true, false, and misplaced? If so, what have you found that helps you deal with it?

2. Do you agree that guilt actually makes us worse parents?

76. No Raving Beauty

1. Have you ever struggled with your physical appearance? What has helped you accept it?
2. How do you try to pass on self-confidence to your children?

77. First Aid and CPR

1. Have you ever been called on to provide first aid in an emergency? If so, what was the situation?
2. Do you feel prepared to handle physical emergencies?

78. Appropriate Energy

1. In what ways do you try to teach your child to accept the consequences of his or her actions?
2. What specific goals have you set for your child?

79. Watching Out for Each Other

1. What examples have you witnessed of siblings watching out for each other?
2. In what ways are you trying to encourage your children to be more aware of each other's needs?

80. Constant Prayer

1. Have you ever suddenly started praying for others and later learned they were in a dire situation at just that moment?
2. Do your children always tell you of a stressful event at the time? Why or why not?

81. Anxious for Nothing

1. What aspects of parenting, if any, cause you to be anxious? How do you handle such times?
2. In what ways do you try to be gentle with yourself as well as with your child?

82. Choosing What's Important

1. Have you ever put off an advanced degree, a move, or a promotion for the sake of your family? If so, what happened?
2. Have you ever missed a repeated message until someone shared from his or her own experience? If so, what was the situation?

83. Tough Decisions

1. In what situation have you had to remind yourself that you are the parent? What was the result?
2. What was one of the hardest and best decisions you've ever made for your family?

84. Alarm Clock Curfews

1. What do you think about curfews for teens? How does your family handle the situation?
2. How do you think your teen would react to an alarm clock curfew?

85. Later Rewards

1. What things would your children say you have done right?
2. What things would your children say they wish you had done or would do differently?

86. Happier Holidays

1. In what ways do you try to de-stress the holidays?

2. What suggestions do you have for those who feel as though they must meet their extended family's expectations?

87. The Contract

1. What do you think about the idea of a written contract for dating?
2. If you were to draw up an agreement with your children concerning their future activities, what items would you want included?

88. Pray the Psalms

1. What helps you when you're praying for your children?
2. What suggestions do you have for parents praying for wayward children?

89. Be Involved

1. In what ways are you or do you plan to be involved in your children's dating?
2. Do you think The Talk is too old-fashioned for this modern age?

90. Decision Making

1. Do you agree that "a decision not made is a decision in itself"? Why or why not?
2. What helps you when you have to make a tough decision?

91. Empty Nesting

1. If you're in or close to the empty-nest stage, how are you handling it?
2. If the empty nest is a long way off, how do you hope you will handle it?

92. Letting Go

1. Do you know parents who refuse to let their children grow up? If so, what has been the consequence?
2. Do you ever find your own parents making demands on you? If so, how do you handle that?

93. Practice Runs

1. How do you try to increase your growing children's responsibilities?
2. How do you respond to the thought "Little loops around the nest will include mistakes"?

94. Thank-You Notes

1. How do you handle expressions of appreciation in your family?
2. What suggestions do you have for those who can't be bothered with saying, "Thank you"?

95. Scripture Puzzles

1. Have you ever been in a situation in which you had to draw on the strength of memorized Scripture? If so, care to share?
2. What creative ways do you use to get Scripture into your children's heads and hearts?

96. Teachable Moments

1. What's your favorite part of the day with your children?
2. What have you shared during teachable moments with your children?

97. Talking to a Child about Death or Divorce

1. What's the saddest situation you've ever had to explain to your child?

2. Based on your experience, what suggestions do you have for parents who must explain a sad situation?

98. One Family's Courage

1. Has your family been called on to display incredible courage? If so, what was the situation? If not, do you know families who have?
2. What helps families through tough times?

99. An Important Apology

1. Have you ever needed to apologize to a child? If so, what was the result?
2. What suggestions do you have for those who find it difficult to apologize?

100. Bragging Rights

1. Has your child ever put your accomplishment into perspective? If so, what happened?
2. Which of your habits will your children long remember?

101. A Bowl of Oatmeal

1. In what ways have you learned the importance of a good attitude?
2. What suggestions do you have for those who have trouble mustering up a good attitude about life's "bowls of bad oatmeal"?

Sandra Picklesimer Aldrich, president and CEO of Bold Words, Inc., in Colorado Springs, is a popular speaker, author or coauthor of sixteen books, and contributing author to an additional dozen, including *Chicken Soup for the Christian Woman's Soul.* Two of her most recent books—*HeartPrints* and *Will I Ever Be Whole Again?*—were awarded silver angels by the Excellence in Media group.

Sandra is a frequent speaker at women's and couples' retreats, military gatherings, college conferences, hospice seminars, single-parent events, business meetings, and educational workshops where she presents the serious issues of life with insight and humor.

Her five hundred–plus articles have appeared in *Focus on the Family, Moody, Today's Christian Woman,* and *Discipleship Journal,* among others.

She holds the M.F.A. degree from Eastern Michigan University but says it is her "Ph.D. in the School of Hard Knocks" that makes her a much-in-demand guest on numerous TV and radio programs, including several *Focus on the Family* broadcasts. She is also the former senior editor of *Focus on the Family* magazine. She can be reached through the contact information given on her web site, www.sandraaldrich.com.